REACH, TOUCH, AND TEACH

REACH, TOUCH, AND TEACH

Student Concerns and Process Education

Terry Borton
Cambridge, Massachusetts

McGraw-Hill Book Company
New York, St. Louis, San Francisco
Düsseldorf, London, Mexico
Panama, Sydney, Toronto

REACH, TOUCH, AND TEACH

Library of Congress Catalog Card Number 70-98048

234567890 VBVB 7987654321

This book was set in Electra by Vail-Ballou Press, Inc., and printed on permanent paper and bound by Vail-Ballou Press, Inc. The designer was Richard Paul Kluga; the drawings were done by John Cordes, J. & R. Technical Services, Inc. The editors were Nat LaMar and Ellen Simon. Stuart Levine supervised the production.

The author wishes to thank the Hattie M. Strong Foundation of Washington, D.C. for its support during the writing of this book.

to my family

preface

This book describes my attempt to *reach* students at basic personality levels, *touch* them as individual human beings, and yet *teach* them in an organized fashion.

I believe that what a student learns in school, and what he eventually becomes are significantly influenced by how he feels about himself and the world outside. I think that schools should legitimize these feelings, and should teach students a variety of ways to recognize and express them. An education without this understanding of self is simply training in an irrelevant accumulation of facts and theories—irrelevant because it is not related to what students *feel* is important. The goal of the teacher should be to help each student constantly increase his understanding of his feelings, and expand that self-awareness by utilizing the vast intellectual resources available to man. Such an education will mean that a student learns increasingly sophisticated *processes* for coping with his *concerns* about his inner self, and the outer world. By stressing the relation between processes and concerns, it should be possible to make school as relevant, involving, and joyful as the learning each of us experienced when we were infants first discovering ourselves and our surroundings.

Part 1 of this book describes the experiences which led me to work on a curriculum aimed at reaching a student's fundamental concerns. In the belief that the best way to explain my ideas is to indicate how they formed, I have described the experiences which convinced me such a curriculum was important. Those experiences are documented with excerpts from my journal, news bulletins, notes, an interview transcript, and an article on my first year's teaching. To explain the power behind the experiences, the students themselves, I have included their voices in poems, papers, notes, and pictures.

Part 2, the major portion of the book, deals with the problems and possibilities of teaching processes designed to meet student concerns. The autobiographical approach is continued, but I have attempted to generalize the teaching principles involved and provide models for lessons that both tap concerns and teach processes. A number of examples show what a curriculum might look like, and a description of other experimental projects indicates a variety of explorations in the same direction.

The transition from the raw impressions of personal experience, to conceptual models, and then to general educational applications, requires several changes in writing style throughout the book. The reader should be prepared to shift gears as he reads, for I have drawn upon a variety of sources in order to define some concrete steps toward a new vision of education. It is a vision in which schools are places that students want to attend, not simply because they desire a job or status, but because their education is important to them as human beings.

Terry Borton

contents

1

REACH, TOUCH . . .

What is there to give
 but giving?
What is there to hold to
 but the gift?
What is there of joy or grief
 but giving?

Giving is the only reaching
 that can touch.

not so much
for knowledge

It was June, 1964, in Richmond Union High, an integrated school of three thousand in an industrial city across the bay from San Francisco. I was assigned to guard the east door during the senior graduation, and from there I watched my first year's students—feeling pride and a certain vague uneasiness. A day earlier they were supposed to have been children. Tomorrow they would be adults—out on their own, off to find jobs, fight in the war, choose a husband or a college. Their commencement seemed unreal. Not school; not life either—an awkward ritual straddling the two.

What difference, I wondered, would the previous years of school make in my students' lives? I did a little mental arithmetic: twelve years times 180 days was 2,160 days, times six hours was 12,960 hours total. They had put in a lot of time. Now, ready to graduate, they were sweating in their caps and gowns, crammed full of English, math, and science. I suspected that ten years later, sweating over a jail sentence, a doctoral exam, or a car engine, even the best of them would have forgotten most of what they had been taught.

I was not overly concerned that they would forget so much: I knew that I had forgotten a good deal myself. I was more concerned with what they would remember. What would be useful, or important, after ten, twenty, thirty, forty, fifty years? That was a question which had plagued educators for a long time and had rarely been answered well. One of the best answers I had ever seen was written back in 1875 by William Johnson Cory, master at Eton School, England. It had impressed me when I first read it, and as the Richmond High orchestra tuned up for "Pomp and Circumstance," I mulled it over again.

> *At school you are not engaged so much in acquiring knowledge as in making mental efforts under criticism. A certain amount of knowledge you can indeed with average facilities acquire so as to retain, nor need you regret the hours you spend on much that is forgotten, for the shadow of lost knowledge at least protects you from many illusions. But you go to a great school not so much for knowledge as for arts and habits; for the habit of attention, for the art of expression, for the art of assuming at a moment's notice a new intellectual position, for the habit of submitting to censure and refutation, for the art of indicating assent or dissent in graduated terms, for the art of working out what is possible in a given time, for discrimination, for mental courage and mental soberness.*

Of course in the Eton of 1875 the student body came from the aristocracy, and the knowledge taught was Latin, Greek, math, and English. Our student body was a cross section of modern America—rich and poor; black, white, brown; well-educated and "disadvantaged." In an attempt to make education more relevant, we had substituted Spanish and French for Eton's Latin and Greek, kept the math and English, and added social studies, chemistry, gym, metal shop, home ec, and dozens of other courses. We had tried to meet the needs of our diverse population by creating a diverse curriculum. We had changed many of the subjects we taught, but I wondered if our curriculum did any better job of teaching the "arts and habits" of an educated mind than did the curriculum of 1875.

Looking at the line of faces waiting for their diplomas, I doubted it. I was even more uneasy because I was not sure what they *had* learned from their school experience or whether it was at all related to what they *wanted* to learn. I had listened to them, but I came away confused. They had come to my class as they were—thirty of them an hour, five hours a day—each a bubbling volcano crusted over with self-consciousness, dark glasses, ratted hair. I had heard those volcanos rumbling in the back of class; I had seen them erupt in sudden fits of temper, in occasional bursts of pride, in flashes of love and respect. I knew that they were there, and I had tried to understand what they were saying to me. But teachers hear many voices—principals lecturing at faculty meetings, colleagues fighting over curriculum, wives asking for more time at home, children shouting for a horsey ride. In all the uproar a year had passed. I had some sporadic journal notes, some moving memories, a grimy collection of student papers, and three hundred seniors to guard during their commencement.

The kids were filing into the auditorium, dropping their chewing gum into the basket held for them by the head of the girls' gym department. I studied the faces I knew, connecting them with the papers I had filed away in the bottom drawer of my desk. There was Charles Thomas, a loose-jointed Negro boy in my slow section, who had written a loose-jointed but beautiful description of himself. There was Adel Caves, daughter of a Depression immigrant from Oklahoma—a roller skating champion who argued about her ideal school as she skated—with elbows out. Charlie Gibbons, a thin, pale basketball player, conscientious even when he was writing tardy excuses. Dick Saunders, black and proud of it, a sarcastic critic of school and of society. Tom Hampton, sensitive to everything happening in a class, sensitive to what the future might hold.

Perhaps those papers, expressing as they do some of the concerns of my students, are a good way to start a book which attempts to suggest an education that will be relevant to students both while they are in school and long after. Even at that first commencement, after a single year of teaching, I was convinced that such an education would have to deal with the students as they were—not simply recognizing their different academic abilities, but understanding and meeting their fear, their hope, their anger, and their joy. What I had yet to develop was a way to make those emotions a legitimate and integral part of the entire learning experience. My attempts at that development —ways to reach and touch students such as the ones who wrote the following papers—are represented in the articles, bulletins, and interviews in the first section of this book. The second section discusses ways of teaching students the "arts and habits" most directly related to their own personal growth.

Who I Am

by Charles Thomas

I am Charles Thomas a law ablie citizen who should have right. I know who I am because there no other one Like me, though I Belong to another and I may not stand a gost of a chance, But I tell the world of Charles, Because He a victim of circustance. If I said I was the only Boy who act this way, then that would be a sin. Im a boy who dream dreames, shall have vision, think, love, enjoy everythink, I am a boy who to self consence, who respect mother father, and other people.

An Ideal School
or
What's Wrong With Me?

by Adel Caves

My idea of an ideal school would be quite the opposite of
the schools in the United States today. I simply hate school,
and as I try to describe an ideal educational institution, you will
see some of the reasons why.

I would love to attend a school much like Summerhill in
England. Just thinking about how free from the pressure and
intense competition that I feel today makes me want to run
away *right now*. How I loath being pushed and tugged, and
constantly made to hurry, hurry, hurry.

School should be a place not only of learning, but of thinking, too. Not the phony way of the so-called "individualists,"
but truly thinking and analyzing, and making one's own convictions. In my ideal school, students would learn and work at
their own rate of speed. If they want to study, that's great. If
they don't want to study, then, that is their business. There
would be *no report cards!* When you take your finals, it will be
evident that you did or did not learn.

I know that I sound like a terribly lazy student, but that's
really not all true. I am just sick and tired of being pushed and
shoved and pulled and pryed at, and I've nearly come to my
wits end. Dropping out of high school isn't the answer, I know.
Really throwing myself into school and trying to be like the
other students isn't the answer either. What is? What must I
do to be able to cope with school?

At least twice a week I sit in different classes and feel like
cursing everyone near me. I get very frustrated especially when
someone makes a remark like, "Boy, you sure look happy
today!" I could absolutely murder them!

Last night I had a very long talk with a friend of mine—a

young man who is only 21 but dropped out of high school at the age of 15. I'm pretty sure he had the right idea when he said, "I know what's the matter with you. You're having a hard time growing up, just like me and everybody else." Maybe all that is really wrong is that I have a bad case of growing pains. Who knows, and anyway, I'll live. At this point I don't really know how I'll manage, but I guess I will. They say the good die young. I'll probably live forever.

Explanation for Tardiness

by Charlie Gibbons

Mr. Rowes, I was late because I had to go by the boys gym. I had to give him my pink slip for monday, because if I did not he was going to take ten points of my grade and if he did that I would flunk for the third period. When I got their he did not believe that it was the real pink slip. then I had to take it to the main office and get it stamped. After I had explain to them why I had to have it they stamped it and I took it back over to the boys gym and gave it to Mr. Larson.

Then he told me that he didn't dout it was the real pink slip but he had to make sure. Not wanting to just walk out on the man, I stood and listen until he was finished. then I ran as fast as I could to this building. I find some old man standing at the door. He asked, "Where is your blue slip young man" I said "I dont have one I am going to class." He said "Why are you late." then I explain the whole thing over again to him. Then he look at me funny like he was trying to tell me he knew that I was telling a story. But he couldn't do anything about it so he let me go. When I got pass him I came on to class and was only about five or six seconds late. After all that I thought I had did good, but I walk in the class room and what happens. You jump on me. I was late but I still say that I am not guilt.

But how long can one keep that courage up?

Our School

by Dick Saunders

The boys went to the boys' bathroom and the girls went to
the girls' bathroom. The hamburger buns were crisp and the
hamburgers were soggy. The milkshakes were cold but too rich.
The bricks were falling out of the building and the paint was
peeling off. The kids write on the bathroom walls. In other
words, the school looks like it's falling apart. The only thing
that is right is that the boys go into the boys bathroom, and the
girls go into the girls bathroom.

Ten Years From Now

by Tom Hampton

In ten years from now I will probably be wishing my past
was not true. In ten years from now I would gladly pledge all of
my material wealth, to erase certain events, that have not as yet,
taken place. And I will be truely sorry for what has happened
then, but as I approach these problems I will not give them a
second thought for now I have a future, in ten years I will have
a past.

culture and concerns

William Johnson Cory's distinction between subject knowledge and "arts and habits" was one of the seeds for an idea which is discussed in detail in the last half of this book—that both logical and psychological processes (arts and habits) can be explicitly taught to students. But when I first began as a teacher, I thought that arts and habits were transmitted by teaching subject content—and in the case of English, part of the subject content was presumably literature of recognized intellectual significance. Indeed, I did not see how "the art of expression" or "the habit of attention" could be learned if the subject content itself were expressionless or unworthy of attention. My first interest, then, was to make sure that even my poorest students read good literature, rather than the childish books which had traditionally been assigned to them.

Just as Cory's statement started me thinking about the relation between content and process, so the papers and comments of my students started me thinking about what it was that they wanted and needed from school. That they wanted something they were not getting from their classes was clear. When I gave them free assignments, they never spoke of the importance of the subjects they were studying. They wrote eloquently about their concern for their own growth, for their classmates, for some kind of control over the forces which would determine their future. But as I looked through their papers and talked with them after school, no clear pattern emerged, except the insistence that I accept the realities of their lives.

I felt that my job as a teacher was to try to connect those realities with good literature. Often I failed, but sometimes I succeeded; and drawing upon those successes, I wrote a paper describing the practices I used for making those connections with the students who were most difficult to reach. Later, after several reworkings, the paper was published. It represents a year's-end assessment of my first attempt at bringing together the culture of the past and the concerns of the present.

CULTURE AND CONCERNS *

The culturally disadvantaged child has it made. He is Upward Bound from Slum to Suburb, his Horizons Highered, his Youth Unlimited, his Poverty vanquished in a recent War.

Such, at least, is the impression the general public receives when the new Crusaders go clanging past. As a teacher of the disadvantaged, I am tremendously encouraged by the genuine interest which lies behind all the slogans. But I am afraid that the new interest may die as the noise dies, and that unless very basic attitudes of public school systems toward these students can be changed, the efforts of a great many intelligent and concerned people may be wasted.

The public school systems' attitudes are usually embodied in a detailed curriculum guide, and it was in that form that I first met them when I began teaching high school English in a large integrated urban school. I could not help being appalled by the reading program for "low-ability" groups. The reading list was

* Adapted from "Reaching the Culturally Deprived," Feb. 19, 1966. Copyright 1966 Saturday Review, Inc.

made up of easy books which preached "good values" but which had no pretense to adult interest or literary merit. Their titles alone—*Little Britches, Wolf-eye the Bad One*—were enough to tell my most ignorant students that they were children, and would be treated accordingly.

In spite of the fact that the classes I will describe here were "low-ability" sections in which the average IQ was theoretically about 85, the students were by no means children. Most had already experienced the extremes of hate, love, and fear. Several had had illegitimate children; four or five were on parole; two had been raped by homosexuals in the reformatory. There were others who shut out the evil their classmates knew and held fast to fundamentalist religion or race pride. And there were some, coming from "bad" backgrounds as well as good, who faced the world openly, and had survived relatively unscathed. The one characteristic most of them shared was that they knew too much about too little, and they had run, as one of my students wrote in a poem on loneliness, "to only here." My job was to reach them where they were and then show them where they could go.

Encouraged by a sympathetic administration, I abandoned the curriculum guide, though not without many heated arguments with other teachers. I replaced books like *Little Britches* and *Wolf-eye the Bad One* with *Huck Finn, Catcher in the Rye,* and *Lord of the Flies.* Each of the latter books was an exciting story of young people, portrayed in a realistic manner, and written in a straightforward style. Each was a book of recognized literary merit with a theme which struck the core of my students' lives. Admittedly the books were hard—all of them had been taught in college—and my eleventh-grade students were only reading at fourth- to eighth-grade level. Yet I was sure that with help they could handle the material—if they wanted to.

The problem was to get them to want to. I began with *Huck Finn,* and after the initial excitement ("He talk like we does")

I met passive resistance. The students did not seem unable to discuss the literature, but they were certainly unwilling. I suspected that the mixed racial composition of the class was behind this reluctance, but the students would not admit it. As I pressed them harder, however, I discovered that racial antagonisms not only were deep but could sometimes control most of my students' thinking. I realized that racial tension was one of the things which had made our previous discussions stilted. Stereotypes and fears were so strong that it was impossible to discuss openly even the simplest boy-meets-girl plot. And when students would not even admit that their racial feelings were important to them, *Huck Finn* was dynamite, and they knew it.

To begin discussion I invited to the class an integrated college panel representing integrationists, Black Muslims, and conservatives. They argued about race among themselves, and once my pupils saw that older students could disagree about race—and yet still not explode—they began to loosen up. One boy finally spoke his mind, and we were off. (The panel, which was invited for one period, ended up staying all day, with dozens of students pouring into the room during their lunch period. They wanted to continue the discussion, so an Inter-racial Discussion Group was formed which met weekly for the rest of the year. The members of this group have been instrumental in setting up a series of concerts and lectures, a tutorial project for elementary students, and a Negro Academic Society.)

In order to build upon my students' newly found willingness to talk about race, I tried to relate their reading of *Huck Finn* as closely as possible to their own lives. I divided the class into groups and asked each to write a short play about a modern racial "incident" in which one race learned something about the other. Each student made up the lines for one character, with whites taking Negro parts and vice versa. The rough drafts were then revised by the group.

This revision turned out to be the most exciting part of the project, for violent arguments erupted on who would be likely to say what under what circumstances. The clash of stereotypes was deafening, but amid the clamor were the quieter notes of realization. ("Nobody'd care much if I married a Chink. Then how come. . . .") The plays were finally recorded on tape and analyzed by the class. One group became so involved that all six of them came after school on the day before Christmas vacation to make a better recording of their play.

Vacation was wonderful. I went off skiing and relaxed, comfortable in the belief not only that my students were understanding good literature but that what they were understanding was changing their lives, opening realms of thought from which they had previously been excluded. My first class after vacation brought doubts again. It became clear that one Negro student had not understood Huck Finn's use of the word "nigger"—a point I thought I had explained fully. I let the class discuss his objection and explain it to him, but I was upset that such a basic concept had missed anyone. It was not until I remembered our first discussions of *Huck Finn* that I realized what a tremendous change had occurred. The fear of discussing race was gone; in its place was an open interest. The narrow personal viewpoint was broadened by a historical perspective. Toleration was replaced by tolerance. My students were still making mistakes, but they were able to work toward understanding.

My own understanding had been steadily increasing. I soon began to realize that race was only one of the factors which limited my students' ability to understand themselves and their society. Discussion of race had been an exciting beginning, but I hoped that literature might offer other ways of broadening the narrow channels in which they habitually thought. Yet before I could teach literature successfully, I needed a way to break up the class hour to keep within my students' short attention span. More important, I needed a way to give personal attention to each student every day and a way to draw out the recalcitrant members of the class.

I hit upon one relatively simple remedy for these problems

when I tried playing tape recordings of the books we were studying. Using a discarded set of fifteen earphones from the language laboratory, I divided the class in half, so that fifteen students listened to the tape recordings for about a quarter of an
hour.

The recordings were as dramatic as I could make them, often
utilizing the voices of my family and friends, and incorporating
a stirring bongo-drum accompaniment played by one of my students. They were designed to give the class a sense of how the
novel should "sound" to their inner ear. I had noticed that my
students read in short phrases, Dick and Jane fashion. Even if
they knew the words, they often did not have enough steam to
plow through the semicolons of an adult style. Sometimes they
took so long to get to the end of a sentence that they had forgotten the beginning. I hoped they could use the recording to
help them catch the sweep and flow of English prose without
bogging down on unfamiliar words. To accomplish this, I had
them read silently while listening to the tape, moving a card
down the page so that I knew they were actually at work. With
eyes, ears, and hands busy, I had them. They had to learn.

One group wrote a short assignment while another listened.
Then they switched, and the listeners read out loud the same
passage they had just heard, using as much expression as possible. Since they had just heard me "reading like you meant it,"
as one said, they were much less hesitant about trying it themselves and much more willing to take suggestions. After five
minutes of reading, we discussed the passage, relating it to the
rest of the book. During the third fifteen-minute period of the
class hour, the first listeners wrote a short assignment while I
discussed the reading with those who had just finished listening
to the tape recorder. These discussions were the most exciting I
had all year with any class, and several times I left the room
with the hair on the back of my neck tingling. For ten minutes
at least I had had the public school teacher's dream—a class of

fifteen, all of whom had just read the material, were anxious to talk about it, and were thinking hard before they spoke.

I usually related the short writing assignments directly to the taped material, and here again the immediacy of the reading, personal attention, and the flexibility of the situation were major factors in producing good writing. For instance, while the first group was reading *Catcher in the Rye* with the tape, I had the other group writing about the reasons they disliked school. As I circulated through the room, I realized that my question had not led to understanding, but had only intensified the hostility the students felt against school and teachers. They seemed to resent writing on the subject because of a sense that their feelings were not quite legitimate. Because they had not succeeded in school, they felt they were not in a position to condemn it. To help the students understand and explore this feeling, I switched assignments for the second group; taking my cue from a dissected worm which happened to be in the biology lab I used for a classroom, I asked them to pretend that they were worms who could see. "What would it be like to be a worm coming up in the middle of a country road? Broadway? A drag strip?"

I wanted to shock the students out of the clichés into which my first assignment had unintentionally forced their thinking. At the same time I hoped to give them a concrete analogy which could be used to show how Holden Caulfield's "worm's-eye view" was revealing and yet distorted. While most of the students wrote on the level I expected, one perceived my underlying purpose. Drawing on our discussion of the book's symbolism, he wrote an allegory of *Catcher in the Rye*.

His worm actually represented Holden, disgusted by the dirt and afraid that society was a ruthless giant which might squash him or "can" him in an asylum. In the book, Holden was also afraid of being "frozen" into society, just as the fish were frozen into the Central Park pond. But in my student's paper, the fish

—those who survive in society—represented a more immediate threat, one so intensely felt by the class that they discovered the paper's symbolism at once and began a hot discussion on the necessity for responsible social criticism and the danger of non-conformity.

If a worm had eyes he would of seen lots of dirt. The people around him would be terrifying giants. He would half to watch where he was going 'cause he easy be step on and killed. His home might be tore up, and he be taken away and put in a can or box. Or the poor worm might be stuck with a hook, and drop threw a hole in the ice and be eat up by the fish.

These sudden flashes of brilliance, understanding, and insight were a constant source of bewilderment. Though I hoped to stimulate them, I never knew what form they would take or from whom they would come. One of the most disquieting of these papers was written in response to an assignment on *Lord of the Flies.* To prepare the students for the symbolic confrontation between humanity and evil, I asked them to imagine the conversation between Simon, the lonely mystic, and a rotting pig's head, representative of the evil which had come to dominate the island. I appropriated a pickled dog's head from an incredulous biology teacher and set it up in front of the class, and the students went to work.

The grisly-minded had a field day, and even Fred, the one kid in the class whom I considered a dolt, was busy scribbling away. I watched him grip his pencil awkwardly in his fist, scrawling words that made a jarring descent across the page. There was scarcely a capital letter or a period on the page, and only a dozen words were spelled correctly. Graded as a conventional essay his paper was a disaster, another failure from a kid I already knew was stupid. But as I studied his strange hieroglyphics, I realized that if the spelling were corrected and the words

respaced on the page, his failure became a striking poem. Dittoed the next day, it startled the class as much as it had me and
stirred an interest in poetry which led to a comparison of Cas-
sius Clay's lyrics with Beowulf and eventually drew the whole
class into composing their own poems.

It was a vine of flies
   on a monster
      that hurt my world.

My friends were Jack and Ralph—
   a world of loneliness.

Jack remembered:
   his world of hatred
   spears ranged
   pig's head.

Ralph remembered:
   crying for me.

And then I ran
   to only here.

I still cannot explain how Fred did it. He never came close
to repeating that performance though he often tried. But from
then on I knew that behind his mask of stupidity lay a mind
with a remarkable ability to condense its experience into a few
poignant words. I could not measure it, and I had understood it
only once, but I knew it was there.

I believe there are many minds like Fred's. I know at least
that many of his classmates were enthusiastic in their response
to good literature. They not only bought many of the books
themselves—in some cases the first book in the house—but
they sought out other books I recommended and brought their
own choices for me to read and comment upon. They were
willing and able to judge a new book on its merits. As a test

case I taught *Mama's Bank Account,* another of the books recommended by the curriculum guide. The reaction against reading such "kid stuff" was intense. One boy scrawled on his book
cover, "The book of non-reading"; another passed in a blank
test paper with a big "F" marked on it, and at the bottom the
notation, "If you give us another book like this one I will shot
you." Discipline problems began to worry me again. There had
been almost none for the last several months, in spite of the impressive stack of suspension notices my students had collected
elsewhere. All of this evidence confirmed by belief in teaching
good literature. However, I discovered that because of the easy
material, comprehension-test grades were much higher than
usual. I asked the students to vote on which they would rather
have: good grades or good books? The result was an encouraging vote for culture.

As I write this article, I feel more confident about the convictions with which I started teaching. I still believe that students who can read anything deserve to read good literature, because good literature speaks about things which are important
to them. I do not believe that clothes or parties or even cars are
the most important things in their lives—all appearances to the
contrary. I have seen them weeping for a dead classmate and a
dead President. At parties I have been swept up in the joyous
and spontaneous rhythms to which they dance. And in the
dean's office I have watched them sulking in anger, desperation,
and loneliness. I hope that I have been able to find books
which will give perspective to these feelings and help my students understand what they feel.

I believe that such a perspective is the most fundamental aspect of our culture and is the way we profit from the struggles
of our civilization's greatest minds. I am not sure that in itself
the study of literature will "humanize"—I have known too
many warped and bitter English teachers—but it does offer one
way to add breadth to understanding. A good writer's explora-

tion of his theme deals with our most deeply felt convictions, and by knowing his work we get some perspective on our own lives. My students desperately need that perspective, and their lack of it is the cultural disadvantage with which I am most concerned.

I know that in itself cultural perspective will not train my students to write standard English or speak an accepted dialect. But without it they have no reason to learn these skills, as they believe that they are caught in a system which offers them no future and which treats them like stupid children. For students in such a position all of life is a nightmare. One of them told me what that nightmare means:

A nightmare is the past, present, and future. I am going to tell you one I had. It was noon and it clouded over and began to snow. The funny thing was the storm came up so suddenly that no one was ready for it. The snow itself was funny looking—a bright red. It kept up for a long time, and the city was buried. When the rescuers came they found people still stuck in their cars.

The frozen people were thawed out and seemed all right, but there was something wrong. It was as though they had lost their minds and had acquired the mind of an animal, like a dog or a cat. Then they found a dog that acted funny when they thawed him out. He started sending morse code out and told them he was a man, and was alive but he could not talk. This was the result of being frozen in the funny snow.

They do not know what made the snow. But if you are ever out and a storm moves in and starts to snow the way this one did, run for cover and stay there until it stops snowing. Otherwise you will end up like me—a dog with a man's brain.

the summer workshop

I learned a great deal about teaching from my experiences in the English classroom. But the kind of things I learned were often defined by the expectations of public high schools. Then I got a chance to run an experimental summer school in Philadelphia—to pick the teachers and students, to determine the curriculum, to make an unfettered attempt at finding out how to meet students where they were and show them where they could go. For the first time I was free to use any subject material I wanted; to explore the acquisitions of "arts and habits"; to talk over an extended period with students about the things they thought were most important.

The proposal for the school was accepted, and in the summer of 1965 the Friends' Summer Workshop was held at Friends Select School in Philadelphia. The teachers were chosen for their willingness to experiment, and the fifty high school students were selected to get the widest possible diversity of races, religions, and socioeconomic backgrounds. Our purpose was to find some way to make that diversity an educational asset rather than the abrasive source of trouble that it was in most so-called integrated schools. We concentrated heavily on art, drama, and English as a way of opening up communication between those who had little in common academically.

Avery Point program

23

We had not been operating long before our original goal of "integration" ceased to be primary. Something more important was happening. The school's concentration on the sociological diversity among the students had created an atmosphere where personal diversity was permissible; individuals began to explode with life. And the fact that we were teaching to a tremendous range of achievement levels drove discussion to basic issues that would be relevant to all students.

The Workshop boiled with a continuous intensity of thought and emotion which none of the staff had experienced before, and could barely control. Weekly bulletins which I wrote to friends reported the turbulent evolution of our ideas and practice as we struggled to bring together the concerns of our students and what we, as teachers, had to offer.

THE SUMMER WORKSHOP

Bulletin #1
July 4, 1965

Dear Friends:

All of you have expressed some interest in the Friends' Summer Workshop. Some are working on similar projects, some have given money, some have given us ideas, encouragement, criticism, and moral support. Besides impressing you at the end of the summer with a fancy report, I thought it might be wise to send you a series of rough notes on our progress, unpolished and as honest as I can make them.

In these first few days Anne Hornbacher and Peter Kleinbard, the drama teachers, have achieved spectacular results. They have organized their course around a series of improvisations which force the students to use all the dramatic skill they have to solve a series of problems in theatrical expression. On the first day, for instance, the students were divided in half, with one group as audience and one group lined up on stage staring. They soon became very uncomfortable, at which point Anne asked them to count the chairs in the room. They fell to counting with great relief and soon discovered that the essence of drama was "having something to do" and that by settling on a "point of concentration" they could loose their inhibitions and convey meaning to an audience. The change in their composure since that first day is exciting to behold. A Negro boy and a white girl can now stand a foot apart and mirror each other's faces without racial or theatrical embarrassment; one couple staged an imaginary tug-of-war which was so convincing that the audience began to take sides and cheer on their favorite.

Paul Keene and Carol Toner have been constructing the same kind of problems within the art class. The students were somewhat aghast when Paul told them that within two weeks they would be painting a picture of a smell, but they are already making strenuous efforts to convey the emotions of fear, anger, love, and joy using white triangles on black paper in abstract design. "Groovy," the students say.

In the English class I have also been attempting to create a series of problems which would force the students beyond their usual thinking patterns. The first day, when most of them were quite insecure anyway, they had to answer the question "Who am I?" in two sentences. Most of them answered that they were "part of the unity of things," "a link in the chain of humanity." The next day I had all their chairs facing the wall, and each student had a number instead of a name. I told them that they had all failed the personality tests they had taken the day before, that they had all lied on them, that their answers to "Who am I?" were humanistic slop. Then, using the "point of concentration" idea which Anne had been developing, I asked them to go out into the city in their imaginations, stare at the

blank faces of humanity, and ask themselves again who they were. The room was hypnotically quiet, and the definitions which were written were striking statements of a new personal awareness: "I am one who speaks out." "I am one who wants to know what I think." "The more I see, the larger I become."

After showing the students Lewis Mumford's movie "The City," we actually did send them out into the city, and asked them to record their reactions to the people around them. One group sat down in the middle of Independence Square and watched the people staring at them; two tried to get in to see their mayor; two tried to find out at the Hospitality Center how to get to know the people of Philadelphia; one girl got talking to an elevator boy who turned out to be an ex-lightweight boxing champ, showed her where his teeth had been knocked out, and gave her his autograph. The students came back bubbling with the excitement of a city they had never really seen in such a way before.

One interesting aspect of the trip into the city was that when we told the students to group themselves, they divided up along racial lines. When we confronted them with this fact in a Friday afternoon discussion on race, they were plainly embarrassed, particularly since they had refused to take a psychological test which asked them to generalize about other races. They dodged around the challenge for a while by saying that the divisions were accidental or subconscious. Eventually they began talking about social conditioning and the necessity to step beyond the circles in which they felt comfortable if they were ever to understand different people. This conclusion was immediately tested in Anne's group, which was meeting out in the public triangle. They were joined by a bum who created a painful silence for a while after he sat down. The students soon overcame their shyness, however, worked him into their discussion, and even managed to extricate themselves gracefully when the bum began to dominate them.

These first three days have been the most exciting teaching experience I have ever had. The students are eager to participate, enthusiastic about their courses, intrigued, and sometimes exasperated by the hurdles through which we have been putting them. They do not always believe that what we ask them to do makes much sense, but they can all see that each aspect of the program is carefully built around the others, that there is a purpose behind the momentary confusion and tension, and that they can trust us not to strike a blow when they are shifting their intellectual positions to deal with new problems.

Next week we stop herding the students during the afternoons and allow them to seek out and create their own activity. We will offer them the opportunity to put on plays, write, paint, investigate the Philadelphia school system, do social work, etc., but the students must make their activity their own responsibility. Their involvement will be the real test of how successful we are, for if the students are actually becoming more aware of the world around them, they will want to participate in it and will be able to find ways to make their participation exciting.

Bulletin #2
July 11, 1965

Dear Friends:

I mentioned at the end of last week's bulletin that I thought the afternoon program would be the true test of the Workshop's effectiveness because we could see the results of the morning's work. I was certainly right, for all our successes and all our liabilities are clearly mirrored in the frenetic activity which has already come to characterize our afternoons.

We began very badly. Monday was not only Monday, with a dozen students out because of the holiday on the Fourth, but it was stinking hot, and raining too. It was difficult to create the kind of excitement we wanted to instill when the students first went off on their own. Nevertheless, Bob Eaton's education study project started off well, and we began tryouts for four plays. We had a request to put on the mob scene from *Julius Caesar*, so while tryouts were going on, I picked an improbably heavy boy and began training him as Mark Antony. Since all the rooms were occupied, we rehearsed on the stairs to the art room. Before long we had a crowd watching, and soon they were talking about doing other scenes from Shakespeare. One boy who had had directing experience took charge, collected the students who had failed to get parts in the regular productions, and is now planning to put on a Shakespeare night which will be completely student-run. Other students are busy writing plays, and Saturday a group was down helping Peter open a children's theater in a storefront on South Street. This type of chain reaction is exactly what we hoped would occur often during the afternoon. If it continues, then I think we can draw in the drifters and keep everybody involved up to his ears.

There have been two major problems which have developed in the afternoon, both the result of the freedom which the students are allowed. The first, misbehavior, was to be expected, I

suppose, and will probably continue to worry us until the students get used to setting their own limits. The second, segregation according to interest and consequently according to race, is a more fundamental problem and perhaps not so easily pushed aside. One of the groups, the Gospel Singers, is entirely Negro, and this is beginning to bother the white liberals, who believe that there should be no differences between races. So far their liberal creed and a closely controlled classroom environment have protected them from coping with interest differences, but now the problem is presented squarely to them, and it will be interesting to see how they deal with it. One of the responses has been discussion—a long one in my class during which the students began to realize that the integration problems of the South were quite different from the kind of community they have been asked to build here. James Baldwin and his conception of a love which can reach across any barrier were mentioned with understanding for the first time. The students began to draw some connections between their problems with integration, their problem when faced with a class without a teacher (I let them sit for an hour and a half by themselves), and the problem faced by Miss Lonelyhearts in Nathanael West's novel of that name. They saw that in each case the conflict was the result of an inability to reach out and touch another human being. At the minute they have evolved no practical solution to the problem posed by the Gospel Singers, but after such a synthesis, I think they may well find one.

The picture of Anne, Peter, and two of their students watching an improvisation gives some idea of the pitch at which the drama classes are conducted. To make clear the difference between a traditional drama course and the one Anne is teaching, I have asked her to write a fairly detailed account of what she is doing, the first of a series of such statements from members of the staff. Anne's course is based on the ideas of Viola Spolin's book *Improvisation for the Theater*, which begins as follows:

> *Everyone can act. Everyone can improvise. Anyone who wishes to can play in the theater and learn to become stageworthy.*

> *We learn through experience and experiencing, and no one teaches us anything.*

> *If the environment permits it, anyone can learn what he chooses to learn; and if the individual permits it, the environment will teach him everything it has to teach. . . . It is*

highly possible that what is called talented behavior is simply a greater individual capacity for experiencing. *

Here is Anne's statement:

Peter and I have structured our course around the exercises contained in Viola Spolin's book, and we have accepted its premise as our credo for the summer. We have been working

* Viola Spolin, *Improvisation for the Theater*, Northwestern University Press, Evanston, Ill., 1963, p. 3. The opening drama exercise on "having something to do" was also taken from this enormously useful book.

to create an environment in which such learning experiences
may occur. There are no facts which will help students become spontaneous in their actions and reactions, no subject
matter which can tell them how to find a sense of freedom
through concentration, no formulas which will help them to
open themselves and to lose the fear of others which is the
source of self-consciousness and nervous tension.

As Terry mentioned in the last bulletin, the drama course is
built upon a series of problems, each containing a point of
concentration which gives the students something to do on
stage. There is no right way to solve a problem, but there is a
self-discipline involved which demands serious attention
from both the players and their audience of players. This is a
mysterious business and I find it most difficult to describe or
evaluate, particularly as I am still feeling my own way and
experimenting with techniques. However, several things have
happened which seem significant to me. Most of the students are slowly beginning to trust one another and themselves. There is less self-consciousness, less silliness, less ster-
eotyped response. Some have amazed themselves with their
own virtuosity; others are beginning to lay aside resistance
and are becoming involved; a few have had the intense and
exhilarating experience of concentration and communication
which the course can hopefully bring to all.

Last Friday Peter and I held our classes out on the playing
field, and asked them to "explore" space as a substance. We
reminded them that they did not exist in nothing, that space
had force and shape and could be molded by action. At first
they were skeptical, but soon all of them were flapping about
making air tunnels and whirlwinds and shapes of all sizes,
much to the delight of a group of elementary students who
were out for recess. When I felt that they had relaxed suffi-
ciently, we sat down in the shade of a tree and I gave them a
problem to solve. Each student, singly, was to build an ob-

*ject out of the "space substance." I encouraged them to dis-
cover the object in the material rather than to start with a
preconceived idea, and I told the audience to watch very
carefully to "see" the object created. A self-conscious girl of
seventeen was the first to attempt the problem. Within seconds it was obvious that something extraordinary was happening to her. Her movements became graceful and spontaneous; her eyes were focused on something in the space before her; her tongue edged into the corner of her mouth. A
shape began to emerge before the eyes of an astonished audience—first the body, then the tail, eyes, ears, whiskers, nose
and mouth of a living cat. When the cat was finished, her
concentration broke, and she returned to us with flushed
cheeks and shining eyes. Over and over, bouncing on the
grass, she said, "I did it. I did it." She was laughing with the
joy of herself, and the delight she had created in us.*

Bulletin #3
July 21, 1965

Dear Friends:

This has been a week of synthesis, or at least the beginnings of
it. The three groups have suddenly begun to feel their identities
and to assert them in a variety of ways. This assertion is evident
in the relaxed rapport between students and teachers, in the easygoing physical contact which typifies the relations between students, in the way the loners are finding ways to contribute.
Even visitors, who have been streaming through at a steady
pace, have found themselves participating and in several cases
volunteering to assist in the afternoons. The integration problems created by the Gospel Singers may soon be submerged in
the creation of a new integrated African dance group which was
formed after we visited *In Group,* a play put on by one of
the Philadelphia gangs.

In drama class, "point of concentration" has ceased to be a concept which applies to actors alone, and now is understood to include the audience as well. In English, the new sense of community found its expression in the spontaneous creation of a group "pop poem"—a potpourri of American cultural clichés which the students chanted through the halls. In art, the most individual of the three classes, students have begun to talk about their work with each other and to band together to help each other in projects. On a recent excursion into the city to get rubbings, for instance, the cooperation of eight students got one of them high enough to get a copy of the Free Library cornerstone.

There are several reasons which might account for this new sense that each individual bears the responsibility not only for his own progress but for that of the group. The most obvious is simply the amount of time the students are spending together —most are here 'til three or four. The discussions we had about *Miss Lonelyhearts,* about James Baldwin's and Richard Avedon's book *Nothing Personal,* and about the necessity of reaching beyond the circles of dead faces have also contributed. But most important has been the fact that each group has been caught up by some project—the imaginary cat, pop poetry, street rubbings—and has felt a part of an excellence which it has created. . . .

Bulletin #4
July 26, 1968

Dear Friends:

This will be a hard bulletin to write. So much of importance has happened to so many students so fast that even now— camped for a weekend's rest in the Adirondacks—I find it hard to understand what occurred. "We began climbing a step at a time; now we've leaped into flight," one student told me as I

left Friday. Many of us experienced that soaring feeling yesterday, yet how we actually got off the ground is still a mystery.

The week began with complaints. Five separate students came
to me with very genuine concerns, so Tuesday I turned the
English class into a discussion of the Workshop's purposes and
problems. Discussion in the first group was vague and relatively
unilluminating. In marked contrast, I was deeply moved by the
next group because they seemed so grateful for their experience
in the Workshop. They felt that they were free for the first
time in their school careers, and that freedom had brought a
new sense of the mystery within themselves and a courage to
act out of their convictions developing there. The question of
"Who am I," which had become a Workshop cliché, was discussed seriously again. One girl said that she had never been so
uncertain about who she was, and yet she found herself doing
and saying things she had never had nerve enough to do before.
Other students talked about the Workshop's "atmosphere"—
the feeling that they could peel off their defenses with which
they habitually guarded themselves and that when they did so,
they found things in themselves which they had not known
were there. We talked about the relationship between individu-
ality and the group, about the pain that seems to be the inevita-
ble result of nonconformity, and about the strength that comes
from once having been accepted by a group of people who supported and respected you even when they disagreed.

After such a response, discussion in the last group was a severe
jolt. The students were very critical of the program. Whereas
the other classes had evolved their own idea of the Workshop's
purposes, these students demanded to be told and, once they
were told, didn't believe the purposes were being achieved. The
discussion was searching, and took our Wednesday night production of Aria da Capo as its controlling metaphor. In the
play, two shepherds make a game of building a paper wall to
divide them. As they become involved with the advantages and

disadvantages of their own side of the wall, the game becomes more and more of a reality until finally they actually kill each other with paper necklaces rather than make fools of themselves by being the first to give up the game. When one student demanded to know who had been killed by a paper necklace and someone else pointed to the boy who had originally led the group, we all fell quiet.

I followed the class into drama. They stood around the bare room looking at each other sheepishly, much as they did on stage the first day. Then Anne sat them in a circle and got them talking gibberish or nonsense syllables to one another. One boy was made to sit on the side and watch. Then the students held hands and continued to talk gibberish, this time with an increased intensity and animated laughter. Anne stopped them and asked various people who had cut the English class, including the outsider, how they felt. The outsider said he felt bored, but hadn't joined the circle because gibberish made him feel foolish. The other students said that he hadn't been invited because they were afraid he would refuse the invitation. Again there was quiet while we compared these answers with *Aria da Capo*.

The "point of concentration" for the day was to teach something to the class in gibberish and to involve the whole group. One girl tried to teach dressmaking and failed. Then Anne made her try again, this time at giving instruction in African dance, in which she is very good. Soon we were all, even the most inhibited, trying to undulate to imaginary rhythms. Then another boy began a Nazi indoctrination session. He lined everybody up, showed them how to deliver a gibberish salute to a picture of Joyce Cary, and demanded compliance. The first girl he chose spat at him. Flustered, he sought another and found a fanatic. But murmurs and ridicule were coming from the back of the column. He rushed back, dragged an offender out, and

began shouting at her. Suddenly, most of the group followed
Anne as she led an attack on him. The fanatic was also
grabbed. It was two or three minutes before the room calmed
down enough so that class could continue.

I left the room, knowing that whatever it is that changes a
collection of people into a group had just occurred. But I
wanted to be sure that the unifying process was completed. I
decided to confront them with a hostile group and suggested
that my next class form a Nazi storm troop to march on
Anne's class. The suggestion caught. In two minutes a tightly
knit column came goose-stepping into the drama class. The response was instant and angry war. This time Anne and I were
really worried about controlling our students.

When we got the groups separated, my class returned to our
room and sat staring at each other. One girl, who had refused
to join the Nazi platoon, was furious at us and violently at-
tacked those who had organized the group and those who had
been drawn in. We talked for an hour. The game *had* become a
kind of reality; the truth of *Aria da Capo* and *Lord of the Flies*
confronted us. Some students argued that they could have
stopped themselves if the game had become too serious, that
there was a "gem" at the bottom of consciousness which
would say no to evil. Others debated this, citing the experience
in the real Nazi Germany. The discussion turned to the techniques of propaganda and mob manipulation. We began to realize that the increased freedom of the Workshop's program
did not necessarily lend to a tidy humanitarianism, that violence and disorder might be released as well as love and creativity, that increased freedom brought the necessity for increased
responsibility for both the individual and the group. We
emerged from this talk—all of us—much wiser about ourselves
and about what happens to individuals when they feel the
safety of numbers.

All that I have written here about group spirit and individual-ism embarrasses me a little. The idea of teaching individualism strikes me as self-contradictory, and I would certainly be suspi-cious of any program which the *Philadelphia Bulletin* pro-claimed "Teaches Teen-agers to Be Individuals." Yet I think that is exactly what has happened this past week. Our purposes have overwhelmed us, and their idealism makes the operation of the program difficult to describe without cant. A description of classroom techniques does not convey the importance of what is happening, and so I end up describing our students and their responses to each other. Their diversity *is* causing us to seek the "structure" of the humanities, the core of meaning which ties the facts together. And that search is exciting be-cause the structure of the humanities is so closely connected with individual freedom, creativity, and commitment to life.

I want to end with a quotation which may help to explain my feelings. It is from Albert Camus's acceptance speech for the Nobel Prize for Literature:

*The aim of art, the aim of life can only be to increase the sum of freedom and responsibility to be found in every man and in the world. It cannot, under any circumstances, be to reduce or suppress that freedom, even temporarily. . . . There is not a single true work of art that has not in the end added to the inner freedom of each person who has known and loved it. Yes, that is the freedom I am extolling, and it is what helps me through life. An artist may make a success or a failure of his work. He may make a success or a failure of his life. But if he can tell himself that, finally, as a result of his long effort, he has eased or decreased the various forms of bondage weighing upon me, then in a sense he is justified and, to some extent, he can forgive himself.** *

* From "The Wager of Our Generation" in *Resistance, Rebellion, and Death*, New York, Alfred A. Knopf, Inc., © 1960, p. 184.

Bulletin #5
August 8, 1965

Dear Friends:

The Friends' Summer Workshop is over. It is too early to attempt a thorough evaluation—too many things are jumbled together in our minds—but I, for one, believe that the Workshop was an impressive success. At its conclusion it moved far beyond its original goals of race relations, which really became rather incidental as we worked with the much more subtle realms of art, personal integrity, and commitment to one's own life. I think we have ended up teaching our students something very important about freedom—that there is no freedom without discipline and purpose, and that that purpose must always be concerned with other people.

Perhaps I can best express myself by quoting a poem, "The Waking" by Theodore Roethke, which became the dominant metaphor for the last two weeks of the Workshop. I read it first in class, and four students immediately went out and bought the book. Since response was so direct, I dittoed it. Again and again, phrases of the poem appeared in class discussions, in afternoon bull sessions, and personal conversations with dozens of students.

The Waking *

I wake to sleep, and take my waking slow.
I feel my fate in what I cannot fear.
I learn by going where I have to go.

We think by feeling. What is there to know?
I hear my being dance from ear to ear.
I wake to sleep, and take my waking slow.

* "The Waking," Copyright 1948 by Theodore Roethke. From *The Collected Poems of Theodore Roethke.* Reprinted by permission of Doubleday & Company, Inc.

Of those so close beside me, which are you?
God bless the Ground! I shall walk softly there,
And learn by going where I have to go.

Light takes the Tree; but who can tell us how?
The lowly worm climbs up a winding stair;
I wake to sleep, and take my waking slow.

Great Nature has another thing to do
To you and me; so take the lively air,
And, lovely, learn by going where to go.

This shaking keeps me steady. I should know.
What falls away is always. And is near.
I wake to sleep, and take my waking slow.
I learn by going where I have to go.

We learned, this summer, by going where we had to go. The
Workshop was experimental in its conception and had a good
chance of failing. But it did not. Almost all of the students
were intensely involved with their work, and their appreciation
for the Workshop was obvious. The program also raised a great
many very fundamental questions about the purpose and practice of education. That is what the experiment was for. I think
that the best way to suggest these questions is to look at the
comments of Peter Kleinbard, the drama assistant. Peter's comments are particularly interesting in light of the fact that Peter
was so skeptical of the program's purpose and design that he
wanted to quit a week before it began and that yesterday he
said he would enthusiastically participate in planning for another program next year.

The last weeks brought to both faculty and students the
awareness that the end was nearing. Many activities begun
even the week before would be forced to conclude quite
abruptly. And so, activity was speeded up. The sense of ur-
gency was evident in the afternoon and evening rehearsals of

three very impressively done plays, Waiting for Godot, The Imaginary Invalid, *and* Slow Dance on the Killing Ground, *and in attempts by the faculty to define more clearly what they were trying to do, and how they could structure their work to achieve the desired end. The week following the improvisation about Nazis we saw a two-hour movie, "The Triumph of Will," one of Hitler's most powerful propaganda pieces. Afterwards the students were led blindfolded from the auditorium. Their willingness to be led blindly was used to illustrate the point that techniques of mass control could be practiced effectively on a group of Americans, even students who thought themselves well able to assert their freedom. The device worked in that students questioned not only their own resistance to enslavement, but the need of a teacher to provoke them in this manner. They began to ask whether they had exercised the freedom we had given them in the Workshop. Why was it necessary to force them to ask questions by creating an artificial situation? Supposedly they themselves would find the need to question their conduct. To what degree are students self-motivated? To what degree had the environment we established by putting together students with widely different backgrounds served to generate questions? The need to use the device seemed to indicate a partial failure, either of the students' response to a challenging situation, or of the faculty to set up an adequate educational environment.*

On the other hand, many activities were operating and succeeding because the students were responding to the challenge of learning about themselves through works of art and through interaction with people from completely different backgrounds. One of the successes was a Shakespeare Program of dramatic readings, organized and beautifully executed by two students. Less formal, but perhaps more significant, was the fact that students were continually discussing what went on in class on their own in the lunchroom, or on the grass triangle near school.

In reply to Peter's comments (to get in a last lick), I think there is no guarantee that diversity alone will create a situation where tension will be constructive. It seems to me that it is also necessary to provide some common goal or obstacle which will force the students together in such a way that their diversity becomes an asset. Production of the plays was such a common goal; blindfolding was a common obstacle.

I think the difficulty we had in integrating the art course into the rest of the program stemmed in part from the fact that although the students were presented with a common problem, they could not solve it either by working on their own or by working together. Art, as opposed to dramatic improvs or discussion in English, is a very individual confrontation with the rigors of a discipline, and until the last problem many of the students found themselves badly frustrated and were inclined to quit easily. The last problem was the creation of a "cocoon" of balsa wood and string which would be large enough for the student to fit inside and would express his personality and his relation to the outside world. The project was extremely difficult. The thin balsa strips snapped during construction; the cocoons were large and ungainly and were constantly being broken by people bumping into them. But the problems of form, space, and stress which the students had been studying ceased to be academic and became infuriatingly personal. Again and again, when the wood broke, the students patched, and redesigned, and reconstructed. Paul and Carol, who had been badly discouraged on Monday, were by the end of the week deeply impressed with the stubborn determination which many of the students showed. They seemed to have moved to a point where they could handle a difficult situation, create something beautiful, and do it on their own, without the immediate support of the group.

Because the cocoons took up so much room, they were constructed at various points all over the school—on the front yard,
on the playing field, in the gym and the halls. These delicate
obstructions, which represented so much time and artistic energy, were in many ways symbolic of the problems and possibilities in the Workshop.

STOP THE
RACE RIOTS

MAINTAIN YOUR COOL

KEEP RICHMOND

FROM BECOMING

ANOTHER WATTS

Come to the meeting at Neighborhood
House at 5 p.m. today.
There will be a discussion of a
boycott, Monday, March 24.

THIS INVOLVES YOU!

stop the race riots

It was hard getting back into the swing of Richmond Union High School after the Summer Workshop in Philadelphia. My principal encouraged me to try to put the ideas of the Workshop into practice in Richmond, but it was discouraging work. All of the regular school restrictions that I had learned to ignore or work around suddenly seemed to get in the way. What had seemed so reasonable during the summer seemed bizarre when done in room 203, and instead of being supported by the warmth and cooperation of the Summer Workshop teachers, I was alone. Even my friends did not understand what I was talking about, because I did not understand it very well myself. And many of the other teachers were skeptical or openly hostile.

Then one spring day at lunchtime, the stark "stop the race riots" flyer appeared all over school. The resulting uproar sucked us all out of our private problems and dropped the entire school on the edge of chaos. Nationally, there had been no riots since Watts, but because our area of Richmond was one of the most desperate in the state, everyone expected a riot sooner or later. All the signs indicated that the conflagration which later became the pattern in so many cities was about to occur in Richmond.

45

A series of interracial fights had broken out early in the week. They spread, and their ferocity increased rapidly. Gangs began daylight looting of downtown stores, the police were ordered to shoot rioters on sight, the National Guard was alerted. The school itself was tense; patrol cars with shotguns and dogs had lined the streets the day before; many of the students carried Coke bottles; knives and guns were reported.

The "stop the race riot" sheet was an attempt by a small group of students to head off the trouble by directing the general anger into an organized boycott of the school. I was in a peculiar position. Most of the organizing students, although operating from a settlement house, were members of the Interracial Discussion Group I had helped start two years earlier. I became deeply involved in helping them to clarify their demands and to work out their relations with the gangs. At the same time I was chairman of the school negotiating committee which met with the students. The pressure of being caught in the middle was tremendous, and I handled it in the only way I knew how—by making myself the most open possible communication channel and ensuring that each side heard what the other was saying. Eventually we worked out a settlement which stopped the fights and looting, made a number of changes the students had demanded, and set up a School-Student-Parent Committee to begin thinking about future educational changes for our school.

The whole explosion attracted a lot of attention, and the University of California Survey Research Center immediately began interviewing participants to see if they could find any pattern which might help forestall future violence. Much of their interview with me dealt with the dramatic aspects of the physical fighting and the complex political maneuvering afterwards. There is no need here to reproduce the gory details of violence—television has made them all too familiar—and the politicking is no longer important. But as the interview progressed, my feelings about what we had just been through began to clarify. The crisis at Richmond High was not simply about integration, or even black power—any more than those had been the central issues of the Workshop. In Richmond, as in Philadelphia, the central question was how to "learn by going where we had to go"—how to make the arts, the habits, the processes of education touch the fundamental needs of the students.

STOP THE RACE RIOTS *

interview

Q. You mentioned before what you considered to be the immediate causes for the crisis. I wonder if you could now go to what, other than the fights, led up to the situation.

A. *Well, I don't think it had much to do with the eighteen points of the students' demands except insofar as those eighteen points reflect the general sense of alienation from the white man's school, and a general sense that white people and white laws and white customs do not apply. I think even among kids who don't create trouble, that's an assumption. They don't get indignant about the fact that a bunch of Negro kids picked up this little white kid in my class, scrawny, 98-pound weakling, you know, and beat him up. That didn't bother them at all. Whereas if it had been a Negro kid, they would be all upset about it. We have allowed a situation to develop in which Negro kids and a large number of Negro adults don't feel any stake in what happens to white people. And vice versa. There is*

---

* Edited from an interview with me conducted by the staff of the University of California Survey Research Center. The full interview transcript was released to me at my request. For a complete analysis of the fights and their aftermath see Robert Wenkert et al., "Two Weeks of Racial Crisis in Richmond, California," University of California Survey Research Center Monograph 21, Berkeley, 1967.

a sense of two cultures that develops in a so-called integrated school. So the Negro kids try to protect themselves and stay within their culture. They put tremendous pressure upon any Negro kid who begins to slide over into white culture. They're riding Lewie, for instance, who is starting to study. That pressure certainly is very unhealthy as far as his education is concerned. I think it's also unhealthy as far as any sort of personality development is concerned. I'm all for soul. But right now black soul hasn't got enough to stand on its own feet. It has to be buttressed by a lot of attitudes and gestures and configurations that are really the antithesis of what's meant by soul, at least as I understand it.

Q. What do you mean by . . .

A. *Soul?*

Q. You can define that too.

A. *When the kids talk about soul music, they mean a singer has feeling which is expressed and has a meaning, as opposed to the yeah, yeah sort of white man's song. If you ask them what the difference is between white music and their music, they'll say white music doesn't say anything, whereas the Negro music talks about a particular desire or feeling. I think more direct expression of feeling is a good value; it's one that ought to be adopted by America. But you know, while I enjoy kids who are uninhibited and have soul, these kids aren't really uninhibited. Look at the defense patterns which they establish—at the fact that they will not allow themselves to be criticized, even when they're wrong. Take, for instance, the kid who, as soon as you speak to him in class, flares up, stands up, and marches out to show that he's cool, he's got soul, and the white man isn't going to bug him, the white man is not going to control him, he'll beat the white man. I think that's a defensive pattern which in the long run is going to corrode what is meant by soul. It's the*

Northern Negro's equivalent to the Uncle Tom gesture of scratching the hair, the shuffle, that sort of thing. The two are built on the same pattern and sometimes you see the same pattern turned upside down. If a Negro kid sees a white teacher coming down the hall and the Negro kid has his hat on, he'll take his hat off and assume a mocking, servile attitude, head tucked under and hat held. It's an underground way of putting down the teacher, true—but I think it's also a way of knuckling under, without admitting that he's knuckling. He does take off his hat. He does it in such a way as to antagonize the teacher and to make him feel as though he didn't have to if he didn't want to. But he does it. What he's doing is Uncle Toming and not Uncle Toming—hardly a direct expression of feeling, and certainly not soul. If soul is going to make any contribution, I think it can't involve running away. And it can't depend on booze or dope or clannishness for courage. It's got to stand by itself, and if it can't, then it isn't there.

To go back to what causes these things: In general, I think Negro kids have developed a pattern of response to whites which is often defensive. That is, they run away from the white man's challenges as represented by book knowledge and the technical ability to handle the world, either by dodging or by a kind of frontal and sometimes rather unreasonable attack. I think there's a general lack of self-confidence among black kids.

That isn't always true. For instance, I have a student who is very cool. And the kids accept him as being cool. He's not a fink. He'll never let you say anything to him that he doesn't like. On the other hand, he thinks he's cool enough so he doesn't have to fight unnecessarily and he thinks he's cool enough so he doesn't have to bug teachers without good reason. That's the sort of conception that I would like to see propagated.

Q. You said earlier that you didn't feel that the leaders of the walkout were really representing the students as a whole. What

complaints do you think still exist among the students that
haven't been answered? Do they have specific complaints, or is
this a general feeling of being outside and not really knowing
what makes them feel that way?

A. *Are you asking whether one could change the structure
enough so that these kids would feel a part of the school? I
don't know. Because the interesting thing is that the white kids
feel precisely the same way. They may be part of the school but
they don't think the school is part of them. They don't see the
school as an exciting place or even in a realistic sense as a training ground for adulthood or as a place which is meaningful to
them as young adults. School is a thing that one goes through.
They say, "Everybody's doing it and you try and do it in such a
way as to come out on top."*

   *Once we were reading Thoreau in class, and I asked them
to go out and "front out the essential facts of life" at Richmond High School the way Thoreau did in the woods. Their
report was pretty depressing: "It's a kindergarten. Everybody's
standing around in groups. Nobody's talking to each other." "At
school you have a laugh. Everybody's trying to laugh or trying
to get a laugh or trying to find a laugh or hiding from a laugh."
But nobody says this is a place of excitement, or this is a place
where people are grappling with important ideas, or this is a
place where people are trying to find out what to do with their
lives, or even this is a place where you study things you need to
know in order to get ahead, although I think that idea is fairly
well accepted. And so what I'm seeking is some way to change
that. I think at the school we ran last summer the students felt
that their experience was enormously important for them, and
that what was going on had a very direct application both in
the short term and the long term. I don't know whether that
can be translated effectively into a full school curriculum or not.
But I think unless it is we'll get a lot of problems that can't
be solved by just tinkering with the system.*

Q. What was it about the summer school that you felt engendered this kind of enthusiasm?

A. *What made the experience important was that we were dealing first of all with an important issue, that is, race, and we set ourselves an extreme case. The school was split racially between kids so as to be an example of our country's number one domestic problem. We said, "Here it is, it's all yours. What are you going to do about it? You've got to make your lives together work in this situation. You're protected from the outside and you've got to work it out." When they tried to run away, we told them that they were running away. And when they became militantly integrationist, we told them they were running away. We were saying, "How are you going to make it work, so that people are just people or so that people are just people with particular kinds of backgrounds and assumptions and feelings?"*

I think the concentration on the humanities was also very important because if you teach humanities the way they ought to be taught, you keep pushing yourself back to basic questions that work themselves out in a number of different contexts. But unless you've got some of those answers or at least unless you see yourself as trying to handle some of those questions, life doesn't make much sense. Most courses in school do not direct themselves to those questions at all. Most of my schooling didn't. As a matter of fact, you could probably put all of it that did into two or three hours. I suppose that's true. Each person can probably think back to a fifteen-minute period or ten-minute period, to one statement by one man that helped to fit things together. What the Workshop did was to try to cram a lot of those periods into a short space of time. There's no question that the kind of thought in that summer school was of an entirely different caliber than what goes on most of the time in school, including most of the time in my classes with what I'm doing now.

Q. It sounds like you're trying to strip off the outside and interact from gut to gut. Or at least to . . .

A. *Yeah, but I think it's more than an interaction, a kind of personal-relations business. That's one thing I'm not sure of, whether what we were doing was a kind of group therapy or whether it has an intellectual structure which was not defined very clearly. But I think it has. I think that it has something to do with this business of the structure of the humanities. That is, if you start any place in a masterpiece of artistic creation, whether it be Michelangelo, Hemingway, Melville, or Shakespeare, and you start asking questions about what's going on, sooner or later you come down to fundamental questions that concern everyone—the kind of questions you have to create your own answers to.*

2

. . . AND TEACH

Teachers can only give so much.
Yet lives may more than brush,
And reaching, touch,
And touching,
Teach each other.

teacher concerns— student concerns

The furor of Richmond was far behind me. I sat with a group of teachers from another school, discussing education. The pause in the talk was heavy with memories. I do not know what the others in the group were feeling, but I was deep in the experiences which have made up the first part of this book—the joy I felt when the kids responded to the literature I loved; the excitement of that incredible summer's communication in Philadelphia; the nagging sense of failure after the walkout in Richmond; the dozens of kids that somehow, in spite of all I had done or tried to do, were never reached, never touched.

The teacher who had been speaking shook her head sadly. "I just don't know," she said. "When I started teaching, I felt I had so much to give. And now—now I know how hard it is to give it."

The room was quiet again. No more words were needed. The catch in her voice measured for each of us the gap between what we had hoped to teach and what we actually accomplished. We were a common enough group of teachers—a talkative home-ec matron, a hard-hitting shop man, a sweet young thing with a Southern drawl, a wizened physics teacher recovering from a heart attack. And our feeling was a common enough

55

one. We realized again—each in his separate way—how much we cared, and how little that caring showed in what we taught and how we taught it.

We knew that only a few of our students had felt that caring, a few out of hundreds. The home-ec teacher had helped the daughter of an alcoholic; the shop teacher had dressed down a kid at a crucial point in his life; I had my poets, my intellectual roller skating champion, my incorrigible characters. All teachers have their pets.

I do not mean that all teachers encourage the "kiss-ups" who try to get good grades through flattery, but every teacher has a special interest in a few students. These pets provide the personal impetus for the vast system of American education. A teacher's conviction that he has "made a difference"—even with these few students—reassures him that education is something far more complex and fundamental than training students to know the phyla, solve differential equations, or speak Spanish. Mere training, teachers fear, may soon be done better by machines than by men, but education requires that intangible "something more."

Stack a man against a machine and immediately the man begins to sound defensive—with good reason. Whatever subject the man teaches the machine can be programmed to teach. The man's knowledge is limited by heredity, personal upbringing, and education; the machine can carry programs built by the most brilliant men in each field, and is limited only by the amount of patience which multibillion-dollar corporations are willing to expend in preparing programs.

And yet we, the flesh-and-blood teachers, feel we have something to give. It is not subject knowledge, or even the ability to structure that knowledge according to its most fundamental principles. The machine may do that better than we. It is not the ability to adapt the subject to the students' own level—the computers may someday be programmed to diagnose each student every day, branch him according to his own cognitive style, retrace the areas he has had difficulty in, and then steer him gracefully into new material. What we human teachers have to give, ultimately, is ourselves—our own love for life and for our subject and our ability to respond to the personal concerns of our students.

We have ourselves to give, and that is a great deal. Within any teacher, within any person, there is infinite complexity, ability to respond, to exchange ideas, and to change personality. The common teacher is not common at all; he is bulging with talent, with energy, and with understanding.

But no one walking through the average school would ever guess it. On a hot day the doors are open; during a trip down long green corridors the dismal drone is audible in snatches: "Turn to page 36 and begin. . . ." "All right now, class, repeat after me. . . ." "When a verb is in the past tense. . . ." "Now what were some of the problems faced during. . . ." "The answer to the third question is. . . ."

If, instead of merely walking through the halls, the visitor did a more complete investigation, his opinion would not be likely to change. The virtues of teachers are not revealed in school. Most of the time even the well-intentioned teachers are bores, their classes dull and mechanical. Of course not all teachers are well-intentioned. A few are despicable tyrants; a few are petty, vicious backbiters; a few are blustering incompetents. But the vast majority of teachers are good people who want to do a good job. If they do not succeed, it is partly because they are locked in a system which denies them their own humanity and the opportunity to give of themselves. The structure of administration, teacher training, and curriculum has turned vital men into repetitious machines.

Within the last few years, a barrage of widely read books has documented the devastating effects of such a system. Sociologist Edgar Friedenberg in *Coming of Age in America* and psychologist Paul Goodman in *Compulsory Mis-education* have struck at the absurdity and acquiescence which schools have generated. The mountain of trivia out of which Bel Kauffman built her novel *Up the Down Staircase* is seen by Philip Jackson's *Life in the Classroom* as a pattern of delay, denial, interruption, and social distraction which may have profound psychological effects after school is long past. John Holt's *How Children Fail* describes the immediate fear which such a pattern generates among children, even those in private progressive schools. Peter Schrag's depressing account of big-city schools in *Village School Downtown* is dramatized by Jonathan Kozol's attack on schools' racism and brutality in *Death at an Early Age*. Herbert Kohl's descriptions of qualified success in teaching his *36 Children* in New York was matched on the West Coast by James Herndon's year of teaching described in *The Way It Spozed to Be*. All of these books are united in attacking what Mario Fantini and Gerald Weinstein, in *The Disadvantaged*, call "the phony school" and "the irrelevant curriculum," and all of them wince, roar, or weep at what is happening to kids.

Casual reading of the daily newspaper gives another kind of insight into the effects of schools. Forty percent of the kids in the big cities never make it through the system at all; mangled, they drop out, or are kicked out. The alienation of those who stay shows itself everywhere. Richmond High School where I taught is only ten miles from the Berkeley campus. It took a year for the ideas of student power embodied in the Free Speech Movement to travel those ten miles, and Richmond was one of the first high schools to be faced with a massive student protest organized by the students themselves. Since then such expressions of discontent and rebellion have become common-place, fed by national confusion of conscience on race and war. Negroes created black power to fight the system; white middle-class kids organized the draft resistance or the McCarthy campaign or opted out of the system and streamed to the Village and San Francisco to become hippies and teenyboppers. Those who stayed home fed their own mass media, the multimillion-dollar record industry, and created a youth culture built on separate clothes, music, hair style, language, politics, pot, and the Pill.

Even the federal government and the statisticians recognized that something was basically wrong with schools. At the request of Congress, Dr. James Coleman of Johns Hopkins University undertook a massive study of "Equality of Education Opportunity" involving 600,000 school children to determine what factors in the school environment affected student achievement. Though his primary interest was the effects of race and social class, he covered everything from the age of school facilities to salary and experience of teachers and for good measure added a few questions designed to get at the students' feelings about themselves and their school. When the statistical analysis of his data was completed, Coleman concluded that of all the factors studied, "including all measures of family background and all school variables, these attitudes [interest in school, self-concept, and sense of control] showed the strongest relation to achievement at all three grade levels." That is, those students who had positive measures on these attitudes had high achievement; those with low interest in school, low self-concept, and low sense of control had low achievement.

This finding appears so predictable that it hardly seems worth spending a million dollars to find it out, particularly since Coleman has not been able to establish whether high achievement causes high self-concept or vice versa. But Coleman's findings mean that the billions that are being spent for higher teachers' salaries, fancy buildings, electronic teaching devices, and new books are not likely to result in substantial improvements in education. If attitudes such as self-concept and sense of control are the most important factor in educational achievement, changes will be required in schools that are as radical as any proposed by the romantic critics or demanded by the students themselves.

They will require, first of all, that teachers begin to look at the concerns of kids, that they try to find out what kids are feeling, what they are thinking about when they are not made to think about school subjects, and what they do with themselves when they are not made to do what teachers want them to. That is not an easy thing for teachers to do. Students have learned from the first day of kindergarten that it is the teacher who is the source of power in the room and that they must be guarded about how they express themselves. It is difficult, therefore, for the teacher to judge how students feel from their behavior in his regular classroom, and the pets he sees outside of class are likely to be exceptional students. If he tries to change the rules so that students have a chance to express themselves, he is likely to run into trouble with his administration.

Even having the freedom to reach student concerns is not enough, either for the teacher or for the students. In my own case, even with administrative support, I did not feel I was making much progress. Although I had some idea from the Summer Workshop of what student concerns were and although I occasionally tapped that level in my classes, I did not understand enough. I had no clearly defined concept of what those concerns could become, no planned sequence of activities which would develop them, and, above all, no time in the hurly-burly of public school teaching to evolve the necessary curriculum.

I knew that student concerns were important, but I was stuck between the alternatives of a jazzed-up English curriculum which turned students on but gave them nowhere to go, and simply giving them the freedom to express themselves. I had stretched the English curriculum about as far as it could conceivably go and still retain the title; the notion of simply providing more freedom did not seem to meet the needs of the kids either. I could not turn, as some of my friends did, to "freedom classes" where the kids could do whatever they wanted, Summerhill fashion. I felt about these projects as I have since come to feel about many "progressive" ventures—that what the teachers had to give was love and what they wanted to teach was love, but since they did not know how to teach it, they gave their students freedom instead. A few students seemed to need that kind of room, but most needed more than being tossed out on their own. They needed help; they were asking their teachers to teach.

The most productive source of that help seemed to me to lie in what I had been calling "the structure of the humanities." The basic idea was borrowed from Jerome Bruner's *The Process of Education* and assumed that there were some fundamental concepts in any discipline which could serve as the core of a curriculum. Literature, I had been claiming, was important because it could give perspective to my students' feelings and help them understand what they felt. For me its structure did not have to do with genre or themes, but with the fact that the basic patterns of student life were reflected, magnified, and explored through literature. That meant that the structure of the humanities was essentially the structure of humanity—a provocative thought but hardly definite enough to build a curriculum around.

A way of thinking about such a structure was provided by a paper I read by Gerald Weinstein and Mario Fantini of the Ford Foundation's Fund for the Advancement of Education.* They outlined a theoretical model for developing courses around the basic "concerns" of students. By concerns Weinstein and Fantini meant the basic psychological and sociological needs of students, persistent sources of frustration and anxiety, continuing emotional pressures, which were always there and were stronger than simple "emotional needs." Particularly helpful was their distinction between the progressive clichés about student "interests" and their own concept of concerns. They pointed out, for instance, that a student might be interested in cars because he was concerned with his feelings of powerlessness, and that the proper approach to such a student was therefore not necessarily *Hot Rod* magazine, but some way of helping him explore his understanding of power.

Weinstein and Fantini were also careful to emphasize that they did not envisage the classroom as a place for solving the emotional problems of individuals; they were not proposing that the classroom become a center for personal psychoanalysis or for group therapy. Rather, they wanted to find a way to direct lessons toward the general, yet personal, concerns of an entire class.

Drawing upon their own classroom experience and the consenses of psychological literature, Weinstein and Fantini defined three broad areas of student concerns: "relationship" (connectedness), "self-identity," and "control." By relationship they meant the student's sense of the relation between himself, other people, and the world. By self-identity they meant the

* Gerald Weinstein and Mario Fantini, A *Model for Developing Relevant Curriculum*, Ford Foundation Publication, Praeger, New York, 1970. "The Trumpet" by Terry Borton in Weinstein and Fantini's book contains a curriculum model developed by the field group working with them. This model was a forerunner of the one to be described in Chap. 7.

student's sense of himself. By control they meant the student's sense of his ability to make himself felt in his world.

Of the three, the one which was clearest to me was self-identity. I had seen that concern erupt again and again—most powerfully and directly in the Summer Workshop around the question "Who am I?" but more subtly in the stories and poems my students had written and in the self-questioning they underwent in times of crisis. The Summer Workshop had been expanded and was beginning again under the joint sponsorship of the public, private, and parochial schools of Philadelphia as the 1966 Philadelphia Cooperative Schools Program. Weinstein and Fantini's paper suggested the possibility of focusing the program around questions of self-identity and beginning to build toward a curriculum of concerns.

toward a curriculum of concerns

At the end of the first Summer Workshop, we had asked the kids to draw up a program for the next year, basing their proposal on what they felt had been important in their summer's experience. Considering how little we ourselves understood what had been happening, it is not surprising that the results of this attempt were jumbled. One group, however, produced a powerful statement:

> *The problem is to break the preconceived notions we have about other people which cause us to know them only on the surface and consequently to know ourselves only on the surface.*

That *was* the problem, though the precision of that description is clearer to me now than it was then. Just as important as the precise statement was the fact that the kids presented it as a *problem*, as a concern for their teachers to work on and teach toward. The following year we tried to meet that problem by defining the educational process involved in helping a student know himself and others "below the surface."

*We want to educate students so that they become larger,
more open, more independent human beings, able to function effectively in a world of rapid social and moral change.
We believe that a person struggles toward these goals
through a process of integrating his thoughts, his concerns,
and his actions. Our teaching will be directed toward the development of this perspective, this sense of an integrating
self.*

We wanted to build a curriculum which would explore the
concern for identity by concentrating on the students' own
sense of the disparity between what they thought about in
school, what they were concerned about in their own lives, and
the way they acted. Though this dissociation of self was revealed in different forms in students of different backgrounds
(e.g., the obsession with "soul," with "phonies," and with
"commitment"), we believed it was a concern common to all
our students, and one that we could build a curriculum to
meet.

Our "curriculum outline" consisted of questions designed to
move the students along a series of metaphors exploring man's
identity as man, his personal sense of identity, and finally the
actions which would express a sense of self.

1   What is human about human beings? What distinguishes
    human beings from animals? Individually? In groups?
2   What masks do human beings use to hide or express what is
    human or personal about themselves? Is race a mask? Who
    am I?
3   What happens when people don't hide themselves? Do we
    mean that we are afraid of being what we really are when we
    say we don't want to make fools of ourselves?
4   What forms will express genuine human relationships? How
    is personal style developed? How can we find actions to ex-
    press our thoughts and feelings, and yet be accepted by
    others?

To explore the first of these questions, "What is human about human beings?" we contrasted human beings with animals and worked out a number of particular questions in each subject area. The whole unit was built around a trip to the zoo. The students were equipped with a sheet which asked a range of questions running from the factual "What foods does this animal eat?" to the more philosophical "Are fur and feathers the same thing as clothing?" "Describe the 'animal' in man."

When the high school students returned from the zoo, another teacher and I put on an impromptu reading of Edward Albee's *The Zoo Story,* and classes the next week picked up the themes which emerged. In drama class the students tested their own body styles by trying to imitate the movement of the animals they had watched—the ponderous stumbling of the big turtles, the grace of the swans. There followed a discussion about why human beings characterized so much of their action with animal metaphors. One girl, who had watched a swan, spoke of it as a kind of personal symbol, but though she seemed to be an extrovert, she could not bring herself to demonstrate its grace in a dramatic improvisation. The swan, she wrote later, was part of her personal dream, locked away in her mental "jewel box" where no one could get at it:

> *I am like a crazy, complicated maze.*
> *I never cry, never love*
> *I am like egotistical egotists*

I am fear, constant fear that they might find out what I really am. I'm not really fear but fear the blanket that protects and prohibits what I really am. I've locked it all away in a jewel box. I'm afraid that it might be hideous. I'm afraid that there won't be anything at all. I'll be disgusted if it's beautiful.

> *My only request is to know it.*
> *When I am dying. Or dead.*

During the session of improvisation in which she first spoke of her swan, she did know what was in that jewel box. She was scared and uncertain about talking, but not disgusted and not dead. Her voice, which had been loud and tinny, became a soft contralto. She, who called herself a "project child" because she had brazened her way through so many special programs, began to take on the serenity of the swan she admired. She was not transformed; no miracle happened; but her response to that lesson convinced us that a curriculum of concerns could make a difference in students' lives.

In the urban affairs class the zoo metaphor was used in a different way. The students took turns sitting on the floor of a "cage" built of circling chairs while their classmates questioned them. "What district of the city do you live in? Do you feel caged in there? Do you ever hear people in your neighborhood refer to people in other parts of the city as animals? Is it better to keep different animals in different cages so they won't hurt each other? What problems arise when people feel as though they're caged in? What can be done about it?"

In a group-discussion period, which I led, we got into a debate about animal and human groups. The class began by collecting a list of different kinds of animal groups (hive, herd, pack, school, etc.), and then I asked the students what animal group their own class was most like. I was unprepared for the answer I got, but I was very impressed: they were like no animal group because no animal group was voluntarily composed of incompatible animals, yet the diversity of people in the room had voluntarily come together to learn more about themselves and others. That answer struck me as extremely significant because it pointed so explicitly to the fact that man's self-consciousness allows him to utilize his own diversity for his own benefit. If a consciousness of self is one of the major differences between animals and men, then one of the most effective ways to make man more human, or more humane, would be to help him explore the significance of his own diversity. And if our curriculum of concerns was bringing students to that kind of realization, perhaps we were on the track of a plan of classroom education which led to our goal of "more open, more independent human beings."

During the summer of 1966 the other questions of the curriculum guide were not explored as fully as "What is human about human beings?" because we did not give ourselves adequate time to work out detailed curriculum. The following year, however, Norman Newberg, who was the drama supervisor, worked very closely with me in planning out a series of units built around our original questions. He brought to this job a rich background in theater and a deep understanding of people and was able to help make the general lesson sequence much more full and complex. Together with other staff members, we began to experiment with additional ways to make our ideas work in the classroom and began to keep careful records of the lessons taught. Slowly we were moving beyond our own classroom experience toward material which we could show others how to teach.

We also began to get a good "feel" for our curriculum. The same kind of intensity I described in the Workshop bulletins of the first year's program was repeated each summer, even though the staff changed considerably from year to year. The same pattern of student interactions occurred, and many of the same questions were raised. As a staff we felt that we were onto something, that our curriculum and teaching procedures were tapping levels of personality which were rarely touched in school courses. But we knew that often we stirred up problems which we were ill prepared to handle in a curriculum form, though our small classes allowed us to deal with each case individually when necessary. Our research also indicated that we sometimes had exactly the opposite effect from what we hoped for—we sometimes made kids more suspicious, dependent, and uneasy —rather than more open, independent, and confident.

The students themselves recognized this possibility and, as so

often happens, spotted one of the causes before we did. Perhaps
the best statement was by a boy who wrote:

The Toad

*Once there was a toad who lived in a swamp. The grown-
up toads at this swamp would push the toad around. The
toad didn't like this treatment but his mommy and daddy
told him that this was good. Once the toad was sent to a
nearby co-operative swamp to stay for the summer. At this
swamp the grown-up toads didn't push him around. He had
fun and was freer than ever before. The toads here taught
him how to be free but not how to be happy when he wasn't
free. When he got back to his home swamp the grown-up
toads started to push him around again, but now he wanted
to be free. He didn't listen to the grown-up toads and he was
killed. Back at the nearby co-operative swamp the toads were
real happy because they had given the little visitor a happy
time, a new experience, and a taste of freedom.*

He put the challenge to us very directly. What were we
doing to make his experience more than "a happy time, a new
experience, and a taste of freedom"? We thought our curriculum outline—the progression from an examination of self to the
study of actions which would express that self—would answer
his charge. But at the end of each summer, it was obvious that
we had not yet been able to do enough. Perhaps the students'
combination of insight and frustration is best revealed in an interview between some educators who wanted to find out how
the program had worked and some of the program's students.
The interview took place in October, 1966, after the students
had been back in their regular school settings for several
months.

First Student: *I sat in school today and it was in geometry
and I sat and I looked at everyone and I*

said, "Now they're really not like I am at
all," because I was so angry. She was teaching geometry—it was nothing. She was saying that this plane is this plane and that
line runs that way and I'm feeling awful
and I was looking at the people sitting there
being their nice little selves—goody-goody
girls sitting there, "Yes, teacher, you're right,
I understand," and they didn't understand
at all.

Interviewer: *Well, what was it that made you feel bad?
That they were responding that way?*

First Student: *No, that they weren't being themselves.
They weren't feeling anything.*

Interviewer: *How do you know they weren't being themselves? Couldn't that have been themselves?*

Second Student: *That could have been her six months ago.*

Interviewer: *Could it? Was that you?*

First Student: *That was me.*

Interviewer: *You mean that experience you had this
summer made you so different from them?
And now you're unhappy?*

First Student: *I'm not unhappy.*

Interviewer: *Well, you're uncomfortable.*

First Student: *I'm uncomfortable but I'm not unhappy
because I think I'm more of a person. And,
you know, I can accept myself.*

Interviewer: *You're more uncomfortable but you're not
more unhappy. I don't understand.*

Second Student: *It's not unhappy, it's just being aware of
                   something. It makes you a little more un-
                   happy but at least it gives you a feeling of
                   knowing why you have this frustrating feel-
                   ing of sitting there thinking, "There must
                   be something wrong with me because I don't
                   like this"—I've been going to this school
                   since fourth grade and more and more and
                   more, every year, I've felt there is nothing
                   for me in this school. And yet six weeks [of
                   the Summer Project] and I feel like I've
                   learned something more than in all those
                   ten years.*

    More uncomfortable but not more unhappy; aware that
something was missing in regular school but not knowing what
to do about it—this girl sounded suspiciously like the toad who
had been taught how to be free but not how to be happy when
he was not free. Many students had similar trouble adjusting to
their parents or to old friends' attitudes about race or education.

    To help make the transition back into the "old swamp," we
held a series of follow-up meetings. When it became clear that
it was difficult to make these more than reunions, we held a
more serious session at a weekend retreat. There we got some
new insights into what we might need to do to make the curriculum of concerns immediately useful as well as philosophically
relevant.

    One of the biggest problems the students had had was the
perennial one of convincing their parents that they were grown
up enough to have more freedom. However, the perennial problem had been exacerbated by the amount of freedom the students had enjoyed during the Summer Project. One boy in the
group spoke of the trouble he was having convincing his father
that he should be allowed to attend rehearsals at a play group

the students had carried over from the summer. We asked him to role-play the scene with another boy so that we could see what the problem was. As soon as the argument was well under way, we stopped it and broke the students up into four small groups. Each group was to go off by itself, re-create the original argument, and then carry it through to some solution. We only specified one thing about the solution—it could be win or lose, but not draw.

The groups came back with a fascinating array of arguments. The students who were playing "son" seemed determined to win the argument and used an enormous variety of strategies. Some wheedled, some browbeat, some threatened. But the one that we all thought was most successful was a boy who began asking the "father" questions about the "father's" notion of responsibility.

"All right then, what do I have to do to be responsible?"

"What do you mean, what do you have to do? I already told you. And you can't go to the play."

"No, I mean what, exactly what do I have to do? Tell me some things that I could do to show you I was responsible."

The "father" was clearly taken aback. "Well," he sputtered, "you, you, you have to clean up your room."

"OK, I can do that."

"And you haven't been doing a good job of the dishes. You never wipe off the sink."

"Yeah, I'm sorry. I forget. But if you feel that way about it, I'll make sure I remember."

"And, and—*why don't you get your hair cut?*"

By that time they were down to the crux of the matter, and the student was able to work out the conditions (including a haircut) under which his father would feel that he was behaving responsibly and would allow him to go to rehearsals. The incident was improvised, of course, but it had the ring of truth. The students had discovered that often it is the seemingly inconsequential things which get in the way of communication between people. More important, they had discovered that asking for particular instances was a practical way to get beyond surface generalities like "freedom" and "responsibility" to the sources of the disagreement.

We were back once again to the statement of "the problem" as the first summer's students had seen it: "to break the preconceived notions we have about other people which cause us to know them only on the surface and consequently to know ourselves only on the surface." We had built a curriculum which met that problem in a general way—it explored through metaphor and analogy the basic questions about what people were like, what made a man a man, and what made men different from each other. We had provided enough freedom so that the students could find out something for themselves about how to get to know others beneath the surface, and we had provided a diverse group for them to know. But except in conferences with individuals we had taught them little that would help them move from a general understanding to action on their own problems. We still did not have a curriculum which could get to the specifics of control, relationship, and identity—a curriculum which could teach students how to deal with a father who was wielding arbitrary authority, how to get closer to someone they were uneasy with, or how to get closer to themselves.

process concerns

A boy was having trouble with his father—what business was that of ours? We were an educational project, not a counseling clinic. We could not go delving into kids' psyches, fiddling around with Oedipus complexes and family relationships. We had a consulting psychologist on our staff to help us if need be, but we wanted to keep our curriculum within the competencies of teachers—skilled and special teachers perhaps, but teachers, not psychologists. And yet at the same time we wanted to be able to teach things that would be meaningful to the immediate as well as the general concerns of our students.

In the follow-up session, we *had* taught that boy something useful about human relationships even without knowing anything about the historical or personal complexities of his case. We had taught him that there were many ways of responding to a situation, and we had found one simple process for breaking through emotional stalemates. If we could develop a curriculum which taught such processes, we might be able to give our students the help they needed. But unless our curriculum explicitly made the transition from literary metaphor to process, we began to doubt that many students would make it by themselves. It is one thing to learn about other ways of living

75

through the vicarious experiences of reading, or even drama. It is quite another to personally learn other ways of *being*. To help students within an educational rather than a clinical setting, we would have to find a way to teach the processes through which they could change themselves. And to do that, we would need a general conception of psychological growth which was useful for educators. To explain that conception will require a few pages which are more technical than those which have come before, but the basic ideas are straightforward enough so that the reader should find them both understandable and interesting.

I an information processing model

The description of human growth we found most helpful is one which assumes that men are information processing organisms responding to vast amounts of data. These data include all the information we pick up—information from books, sensations like the smell of cookies and the feel of flesh, inner images like towers and psychedelic spots, feelings like loneliness and love. We respond to these data through processes. A process is *a way of doing* that has form and structure, a way of operating, a purposive behavior. Processes allow us to connect the information we receive to new responses—actions, dreams, feelings, thoughts.

The information processing approach has a rich background in recent psychological literature,* but the amount of theoretical

---

* *Organismic Psychology and Systems Theory* by Ludwig von Bertalanffy (Barre Publishers, Barre, Mass., 1968) gives a short, straightforward description of the assumptions of an information processing, or "systems theory," approach to human development and its implications for various kinds of human endeavor, including education. *Cybernetic Principles of Learning and Educational Design* by K. U. Smith and M. F. Smith (Holt, New York, 1966) pulls together a fascinating though somewhat confusing collection of experiments and applications involving an information processing, or "cybernetic," ap-

complexity which it is possible to translate into classroom practice is at present rather small. We used the theory because it was suggestive, but we kept the model from which we worked a very general one that could be helpful in organizing our work and yet not be prescriptive.

We began with the simple stimulus-response diagram used by the behaviorists. Here the organism is viewed as a "black box" about which nothing need be known in order to influence behavior. Changes in behavior are seen as a function of the stimulus and the way the response is reinforced. Reinforcement of a particular response is usually accomplished by rewarding its occurrence, as by giving a grain of corn to a pigeon when it pecks a bar or giving praise to a boy who responds correctly to a programmed text.

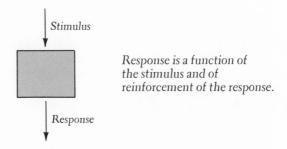

Stimulus

Response is a function of the stimulus and of reinforcement of the response.

Response

proach. *Cognitive Psychology* by Ulric Neisser (Appleton-Century, New York, 1966) is a readable summary of some of the recent research about the inner processes of the brain. *Six Psychological Studies* by Jean Piaget (Vintage Books, Random House, Inc., New York, 1968) contains several essays in which the famous genetic epistemologist explains how cognitive and affective development result from cybernetic interactions between man and his environment. *Process as Content* by J. C. Parker and L. J. Rubin (Rand McNally, Chicago, 1966) suggests several curriculum applications of the processing approach which are similar to the one presented here, and *New Priorities in the Curriculum* by Louise Berman (Charles E. Merrill Publishing Company, Columbus, Ohio, 1968) contains an extensive bibliography on the subject.

We expanded this basic model by opening up the black box to suggest more interaction with the environment, and by hypothesizing three basic information processing functions within it:

1 A Sensing, or perceptual, function which intuitively picks up information, or stimuli.
2 A Transforming function which conceptualizes, abstracts, evaluates, and gives meaning and value to the sensed information.
3 An Acting function that rehearses possible actions and picks one to put out into the world as an overt response.

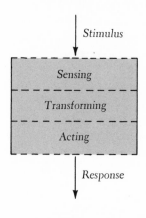

Stimulus

Sensing

Transforming

Acting

Response

Response is a function of the stimulus, of reinforcement, and of intermediate processes.

The model's three divisions are arbitrary, for the processes do not function in a simple 1–2–3 sequence, but are interwoven in a dynamic fashion. Nor do the processes correspond to biological phenomena, for not enough is yet known about how the brain functions to make that correspondence. The model is limited by science's limited knowledge, but it provides a workable way of thinking about the processes of the human mind, and of building a curriculum to make them more explicit.

An example from an ordinary life situation will clarify how

the model depicts the information processing flow. The information may come from an outside source, such as a clock on the wall telling us we are late for an appointment, or from the mental irritation which being late produces. Thus we may Sense the information with our eyes or become aware of our own anger. We may Transform it, depending upon our value orientation, by making up excuses for ourselves, blaming someone else, or simply accepting our tardiness. And we may express this transformation in either mental or physical Action by swearing to ourselves, cursing someone else, or shaking our head in sad acknowledgment that we are late once again.

The person using these processes is not governed solely by the nature of the stimulus and/or reinforcement of the response (as in behaviorist theory) but is also influenced by *feedback* on how successfully he is achieving his own goals.

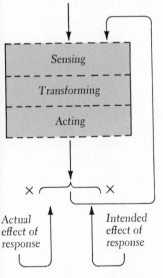

awareness of the difference between his response, its actual effect, and the intended effect, forms feedback which can be used to modify behavior.

This feedback is a man's own awareness of the relation between his response, the actual effect of his response, and the intended effect. If the actual effect (as he perceives it) is as he intended, then the feedback will be that he is "right on target." If his response does not get the effect he intended, then he will know that he needs to modify his behavior until he achieves his goal.* Thus the feedback process allows a man to change to meet the requirements of his changing environment. If he and the environment are fairly stable, then relatively minor reassessments will be needed to keep him functioning adequately. If, however, either he or the environment changes drastically, then the feedback system will be thrown into disequilibrium, and in order to get back on a track which is satisfying to him, he may have to find ways to completely change his response, his intended effect, or the effect he actually has.

The difference in the amount of change required is one of degree, but meeting any change creates some concern in the individual, because he can never be sure he will meet it adequately. Eric Hoffer, whose eventful life has included experiences ranging from manual labor to being a university professor and serving as a President's philosopher, describes in *The Ordeal of Change* how even the most insignificant changes can produce anxiety:

Back in 1936 I spent a good part of the year picking peas. I started out early in January in the Imperial Valley and drifted northward, picking peas as they ripened, until I picked the last peas of the season, in June, around Tracy. Then I shifted all the way to Lake County, where for the first time I was going to pick string beans. And I still remember how hesitant I was that first morning as I was about to

* The model as it is drawn here is technically what is called a "closed" system—that is, a system in which all the processes and the relations between them are specifiable, so that the system's total behavior is the sum of its parts. Clearly people do not operate this way, but are "open" systems—unspecifiable, interactive, organismic, more than the sum of their parts. We have found the closed-system model helpful as a first suggestive approximation for curriculum building, but we are giving increasing attention to how the characteristics of an open system may be employed in educational theory.

address myself to the string bean vines. Would I be able to
pick string beans? Even the change from peas to string beans
*had in it elements of fear.**

Through a lifetime of responding to new situations, big and
little, performing successfully in some and unsuccessfully in
others, each of us generalizes his emotional response to change
into three broad areas. These areas (the "concerns" outlined by
Weinstein and Fantini) stem from the interaction of a conscious information processing organism with its surroundings:
its relation to its environment, its control over its own direction, and its awareness of self. The concern for *relationship* develops because men depend on relationships, particularly with
other people, for all the information which allows them to survive. The concern for *control* develops because men want to
control enough of their relationships to ensure their own life
and growth. And the concern for *self* develops because men are
not only aware of their interactions with the environment but
also aware of being aware, and constantly evaluating their own
role in the interaction.

The immediate situations which tap these generalized concerns and feed into them may or may not be threatening. If they
are threatening, then they will be *problems* which have to be
solved, and the man with the problems will of course be concerned about them in a much more immediate way than he is
concerned about self-identity or control. A particular problem
could be almost anything—a girl, a book, a war, a loss of faith
—anything. But if that problem is handled badly, then the resulting sense of inadequacy will become generalized into increased anxiety about self, relationships, and control which will
affect the ability to respond when the next problem arises. Con-
versely, if the processes can be found to handle the problem,
there will be increased confidence in the ability to handle new
situations in the future.

* New York, Harper & Row, 1963, p. 3.

If the immediate situation is not threatening and the actual effect of an individual's response is not so far from his intended effect as to scare him, then he will believe that he (his information processing system) is operating well, and he will have no particular anxiety about his self-identity, relationship, or control. Perhaps he will sit in relatively quiet satisfaction. But more likely, given the evidence that men seek some stimulation and change, he will extend himself to those *interests* which will reaffirm his own sense of himself, his relationships, and his control. He may explore himself through drugs or by writing poetry; he may become increasingly interested in his relationships with women or with his business associates; he may test his own self-control on the ski slopes, in financial speculating, or in intellectual argument.

Concerns, then, can be related to either a student's problems or his interests, and whether a particular situation is a problem for him or a source of interest will depend in large part on how effectively he is capable of responding to it. That is, the ease of his response will depend on whether he knows appropriate processes for handling the situation—whether our Summer Project student knows the process of "specifying behaviors" to handle his father, or whether Eric Hoffer knows "the bean-picking process" for being a migrant laborer. Because concerns develop from an information processing system and because they can be met by developing new processes to cope with changing personal and social situations, we call them "process concerns."

2 curriculum implications

If concerns are thought of as process concerns, as being a function of *ways of experiencing*, rather than of precisely what is experienced, then there are profound consequences for building a "curriculum of concerns." First, the purpose of such a curriculum should be to teach students new processes, new ways of experiencing—new ways of Sensing, Transforming, Acting, and obtaining feedback. If this is the purpose, then the particular subject matter used becomes less important than what it teaches about processing functions. This is another way of putting what William Johnson Cory meant, in the passage quoted earlier, when he said that one went to a great school "not so much for knowledge as for arts and habits." Information processing language is useful because it helps to specify what ought to be done to obtain that end. At William Johnson Cory's Eton of 1875 (and until very recently), thousands of students were required to take Latin, not for its own sake or even because it formed the root derivations of many English words (learning a hundred Latin words would cover most important roots), but because the Latin system of conjugations and declensions was supposed to give the student an "organized mind." There is no evidence that this happened; in fact four years of Latin may have contributed to quite a few scrambled heads. But if the objective was to teach students the *process* of organizing data systematically, then the information processing approach suggests that that process could have been taught quite explicitly, and the student helped to apply it to many situations besides the one he learned it in.

Similarly, in the psychological area, if the objective of our summer program was to help students be "more open, more independent human beings," we needed to define as precisely and fully as possible what processes that goal would entail and then teach them in the most explicit and transferable way possible. Teaching them does not mean simply preaching, though some direct statement is probably necessary. It means involving students in such an immediate and experiential way that they realize that they need a particular process, analyze how it works, and then apply it.

For instance, one of the processes involved in being a more open, independent human being is the process of getting outside of one's self fully enough to understand what it means to be another human being. In order to teach such a process, the teacher might label it "getting outside yourself" or "shifting perspective" and describe it as an intellectual concept. Then the students might role-play a topical situation which was close to their problems and interests—a racial fight, for instance, or a fight between the academic and vocational kids. Students would first choose which side they wanted to be on and would then reverse sides, so that they would have to act out of an intuitive understanding of an entirely different personal and social self. Then the class would be asked to analyze what they had been doing, assess what subprocesses had been helpful in making their intuitive leap, explore the meaning of using such processes, and determine what value systems they imply. Finally, they would be asked to reapply their new understanding of the "getting outside yourself" process—perhaps first by role-playing another argument while consciously trying to understand the perspective of their opponent and then by using the process outside of the classroom and reporting back on the results.

A curriculum which defines processes and teaches them in such an explicit and experiential fashion avoids many of the problems which were generated by the Summer Projects when we tried to "turn kids on" by teaching directly to their concerns for self-identity, relationship, or control. Bringing such concerns to the surface without providing a means (a process) for dealing with them can turn a curriculum of concerns into a curriculum of anxiety. Such a curriculum may reach things which are important to students. But it offers no hope of coping with concerns and little possibility for teaching the students how to deal with their anxiety other than by exploring it and learning that other people share similar feelings. It is not surprising that such a curriculum might produce depression and frustration, especially when the students have to face "the real world." A curriculum for process concerns, however, is a curriculum for change. It meets the student's need to learn the processes through which he can modify his habitual patterns of response and increase his alternative ways of meeting and changing his environment. As long as he can handle this constant interaction between a changing self and a changing environment, process concerns will be positive concerns—and the learning of new processes will be a joyful and exciting experience.

The concept of process concerns takes the curriculum out of the context of those psychologies which emphasize past experience buried in the unconscious and moves it into the realm of the here and now. This shift from past to present is extremely important for the teacher, most obviously so in the case of the ghetto teacher. For no matter how much he wants to, the ghetto teacher cannot do anything about his students' past, and little about the present which exists for them outside of his classroom. The only part of the child's life on which he has any immediate impact is what is happening right in his classroom. If he wishes to help his students, he must find a conception of them which will allow them to take what they learn in the class and apply it on their own.

A curriculum based upon process concerns does not require that the teacher work through the particular interests or emotional problems of 150 single individuals—the kind of problem which would be better handled by personal counselors. The curriculum may deal with real and immediate problems as a starting point, but no miracles of solution or dramatic changes are expected or required. The curriculum's purpose is to teach an understanding of the process of change, to give the student practice in using it, and to instill confidence that he can go about the business of changing himself in his own time and as he sees fit.

Finally, a curriculum for process concerns does not require the outside manipulation of reinforcement contingencies. A curriculum built on process concerns is based directly on one of man's defining characteristics—his consciousness of himself. Reinforcement is used whenever it proves effective, but not without making students explicitly aware of how it is operating. For it is *consciousness*, a man's ability to step aside from his

own experience and view it objectively, which must be trained
if a student is to learn how to generate his own new alternatives
to a changing social and personal world.

3 a process-curriculum model

A curriculum for process concerns must move back and forth
between the concern caused by a particular problem or interest
and the processes which can make that concern a source of
growth. First, it must find out *what* particular content reaches
students and then teach so as to expand their understanding.
Second, this teaching must help students learn *how* to develop
alternative processes for handling themselves, other people, and
their environment so that they can increase the personal options open to them.

The first section of this book describes a number of attempts
to find what curriculum content reaches and touches students
where they are. There is no need to recapitulate those ideas
here, except to abstract some generalities. Part of the relevant
curriculum must come from the students themselves and from
the particular problems or interests which they bring to the
classroom—race, for instance, or sex or drugs. The students are
as they are. Teachers must see who is there and accept the importance of each student's life. Unfortunately this is not as obvious as it sounds; denying the reality of student life is a common form of educational neurosis. But while it is important to
face student problems, that does not mean restricting the curriculum to what the students already know. It is insane to use
materials which pretend that slums do not exist if the students
live in a slum; it is ridiculous to limit the curriculum to a discussion of garbage and rats. The content of a curriculum of concerns should be as rich and diverse as the knowledge, feeling,
and behavior of all mankind. It should give students, no matter
who they are, the widest possible perspective on their own problems and interests.

The second requirement for a curriculum of concerns—that it give each student a sense of how he may continue to grow within himself and within his world—depends on utilizing a student's consciousness of his own information processing system. It is consciousness of himself and his environment which produces his concerns; it is also consciousness which can serve as the tool to make those concerns a source of expanded possibility. Consciousness produces concerns because it allows a student to step outside his own experience and question it, but it also allows him to step outside his *way of experiencing* and question that. The information processing system can be turned consciously in on itself and used for self-generating growth.

In daily life we sometimes operate this way, though usually because someone has made a remark to us which reveals something we did not know about ourselves and so works the feedback process for us. Suppose that someone says our invariable good cheer (our response) is phony and irritates people (the actual effect) because we keep it up even when other cues indicate that we are furious. We may begin to wonder whether or not they are right, start watching ourselves, and discover that we have, in fact, built up the idea that always being cheerful is the best way to get what we want (our intended effect). Upon analyzing this feedback, we may decide that our behavior does not fit with other ideals we hold about honesty and sincerity and so begin to experiment with new patterns of behavior. The same pattern of natural feedback might help us improve our problem-solving processes in a more academic sphere of activity, and it is in this way that most of our pre- and post-school learning occurs.

A curriculum of process concerns works in a similar fashion, except that the process is more explicit and thorough than in ordinary life, where it is likely to be vague and accidental. Its purpose is to intentionally turn the information processing system in on itself and so to increase a student's understanding of the processes through which he handles information. Diagrammatically, this rather complicated-sounding operation can be represented very simply by building on the earlier information processing model. Because the three functions of Sensing, Transforming, and Acting are intentionally utilized, they are pulled to one side of the diagram and made part of the conscious feedback about the effectiveness of the response.

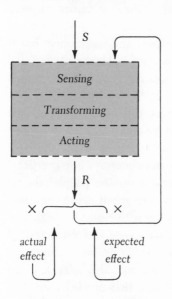

Sensing	Transforming	Acting
What	So What	Now Wha

Sensing, Transforming, and Acting are now intentional processes, being consciously used to generate feedback which will help determine how effectively the regular processing system is functioning. In building curriculum, we found that an effective way to think about each of these intentional processes was to use the colloquial question which best seemed to catch its meaning: "What?" for Sensing out the differences between response, actual effect, and intended effect; "So What?" for Transforming that information into immediately relevant patterns of meaning; "Now What?" for deciding on how to Act on the best alternative and reapply it in other situations. This What, So What, Now What sequence became the model on which we built a curriculum designed to make students more explicitly aware of how they function as human beings.

Though the What, So What, Now What sequence can take many different forms, extensive examples of which will be discussed later, an immediate example may clarify the curriculum model. If, for instance, a student is overly suspicious, then he must first discover What he is doing, perhaps by becoming immersed in a role-playing exercise so that he can see the pattern of his behavior emerge there. He will then need to begin asking, "So What?" What difference does his behavior make? What meaning does it have for him, and what are its consequences? Finally, he will need to ask, "Now What?" Now that he sees that he is suspicious, what does he want to do? How can his new understanding be translated into new patterns of behavior? Does he want to experiment with a more open attitude, assess its consequences, and reapply what he has learned?*

We have found that a curriculum based on the What, So What, Now What sequence and addressed to process concerns works best if the What, So What, Now What questions are asked in two quite different manners. The first is the *analytic* mode with which most of us are familiar—hard-driving, pointed, sharp, logical, tough, and rigorous. But it is difficult for people to change if they are put under much pressure, so we also employ a *contemplative* mode, a more relaxed approach which avoids picking at one's self and allows alternatives to suggest themselves through free association and metaphor. The combination of the two modes creates an effect similar to that which a person experiences when hours of difficult work on a problem get him nowhere and then suddenly the missing link pops into his head while reading Dr. Seuss to the children. The

---

* "Process Education: The What, So What, Now What Sequence" by Terry Borton (McGraw-Hill Sound Seminars, 330 West 42nd St., New York, N.Y., 1969) is a half-hour audio tape discussing this model. To illustrate the sequence, the audience members are asked to participate in a hand-shaking exercise which makes them conscious of their own behavior, its implications, and how it can be changed.

juxtaposition of pressure and relaxed support produces the result. Similarly, our purpose is to utilize both the logical, analytic, cognitive processes and the prelogical, psychological, intuitive processes—bringing both to bear upon the dynamics of self-change.

The What, So What, Now What sequence using both the analytic and contemplative modes of inquiry can be used to build a tremendous number and variety of curricula. The same model can be used to design a semester's course, a unit within the semester, or a lesson within the unit. But like the Sensing, Transforming, Acting, feedback model on which it is based, it does not purport to have life relegated to a stark and unchanging pattern. There are processes within processes and cycles within cycles. The reason for keeping the model simple is to create a framework within which to sort out the mass of confusing data in the classroom and so move toward more conscious examination of the processes through which we order our world.

All of us are constantly involved in this business of learning more about ourselves. Sometimes the learning takes place in an instant—one of those "clicks" or "wows" when everything seems to fall joyfully into place; sometimes it takes a lifetime of painful struggle. But in a society where the social environment is changing with incredible speed, such learning cannot be left to accident. More and more we will require an explicitly acquired ability to consciously change patterns of information processing while maintaining a sense of self. If we cannot accomplish this change, we may remain ourselves, but we will find ourselves irrelevant—unable to influence the world around us and perhaps unable to survive.

Those who can change and who can adapt themselves to meet the changing problems which life presents them do not necessarily become great and famous men—that is a function of luck, ambition, and a host of other variables. But they do become great people. They are the ones in every class and socioeconomic group to whom the rest of us go for advice. We do not go to them because they are always right, but because they seem to have an understanding of their lives which helps us to clarify our own. I believe that one of the purposes of education is to produce more of these great people—people who have developed a conscious grasp of the processes through which they themselves grow. A curriculum with that goal educates man in his own humanity, in his power to change his life by changing the processes he uses to form himself.

CHAPTER EIGHT

applying the
process approach

The Greeks inscribed "Know thyself" above the Delphic oracle. Shakespeare had Polonius tell his departing son, "This above all, to thine own self be true." And in "Self-reliance" Emerson wrote, "Trust thyself; every heart vibrates to that iron string."

Know thyself, be true to thyself, trust thyself—these have been among the great themes of sages throughout history. Yet self-knowledge—knowledge of one's own concerns and processes —is as difficult to obtain as it is powerful, and usually has been won by relatively few people. It may be some time before many of us can reach the insight of those few, but all of us could improve our knowledge of self and would benefit from doing so. The What, So What, Now What model for process education is a means to that end. It provides an organized way of increasing awareness (What), evaluating intention (So What), and experimenting with new behavior (Now What).

The same sequence can also be used to explore process operation in academic areas such as science and math. Indeed, scientific experiments follow almost exactly the same progression—observing data, building interpretations, applying the interpretations, and checking the results—a continuous cycle of inquiry. But because traditional subject areas receive so much attention in our present schools, I have concentrated this discussion of the model's application on the vital, yet neglected areas of self-knowledge and personal growth.

The model begins to suggest how to build lessons that lead to greater conscious control of the Sensing, Transforming, Acting processes, but it is still very general. It means very little, after all, to teach a student to "Sense better" or "Act better." To move from the model to actual lessons takes a precise definition of what processes are to be taught. Although some suggestions for developing such specific processes and some examples of them are given later, the examples which make up the bulk of this chapter have been kept fairly general in order to give an overall sense of how processes can be taught. The lessons used as examples are not meant to be related to one another, but they do represent concrete examples of various approaches at different grade levels, ranging from improvisation in high school to a printed child's reader and from very explicit lessons to metaphoric ones. Some general rules of methodology are woven into the specific discussion of each lesson.

First, some introductory comments: Even these examples will not fill in the model very precisely. The What, So What, Now What sequence represents a fluid process. No part of it can exclude another; no part is more important than another. We can all think of teachers who act as if a part of the process were the whole—those sentimentalists who are obsessed with what they are experiencing, those cognitive demons who ask endless So whats, or the activists who confuse perpetual motion with change. *The What, So What, Now What sequence should be a continuous integrated flow.* Do not expect students to begin at some "beginning" and end at some "end," for beginning at any point should lead back through the same sequence. Start where the students are, and pick up the other parts of the process as they seem appropriate. If the sequence no longer seems helpful in a real situation, then abandon theory and follow intuition. The model, after all, grew out of attempts to system-atize intuition; its validity does not rest on empirical or scien-tific proof, but on its usefulness in real situations. *When the model does not prove useful, change it.*

Even if the What, So What, Now What sequence is treated as a flow, it has its own special problems and opportunities:

what

An experience causes the student to make a response in a situa-tion where he can be helped to examine its actual and intended effects and the kinds of concerns which it raises. The experi-ence should involve things which are close to the student and raise concerns in a very direct fashion, or the process to be taught will seem an obvious cliché with no importance. If the experience is a "hot" one which gets kids talking about what is important, then the teacher has an opening onto a deeper level and can show kids how the processes can be used to help work out their concerns. It is vital not to duck concerns about race, sex, power, or anything else that students find important. If the process will not work on the things that concern them, then they will never believe that it is worth learning, and they may well be right.

The What phase of a lesson often produces a good deal of fun and uproar—if the experience is a good one, the kids will be involved in it, and that probably means they will be talking and laughing. But contemplation and analysis cannot be conducted in such a setting. *Quiet down the classroom for the So What stage.* The transition between the What and So What will be easier for the students to take seriously if the teacher makes it clear ahead of time that the rules for the class are going to change during the hour. There is no reason why a process edu-cation need be chaotic. Students should use the freedom of the What experience for a purpose, not for horsing around, and they are perfectly capable of understanding this distinction if the teacher means it. The transition to the So What stage will go more effectively if the stepping aside from fun and uproar is dramatic and physical. For instance, the seating pattern can be changed to a tight circle with the teacher taking a prominent position, there can be clear rules for discussion, one at a time, hand raising, etc.

so what

The So What stage is close to what a good teacher might normally do with an English or social studies class, except that the focus of attention is the experience which the students have just had. *The So What stage is rational, intellectual, cognitive —a delving into the meaning of what has just happened* as that meaning is interpreted through the many different value systems of the students in the class. In the So What stage it is particularly useful to employ two different modes of approaching a problem—analysis and contemplation. *Analysis is useful because it clarifies meaning and intention, but it must be used sparingly.* An incessant "Well, so what?" can dissect a feeling, a value, or a rational structure to the point of disintegration. *Contemplation allows a more relaxed approach to the problem, where values and meanings are allowed to suggest themselves rather than be driven into a corner.*

now what

The Now What phase is the most difficult of all and requires the greatest skill from the teacher. Here the teacher must take the concerns which were raised earlier (slightly different for every class), mesh them with the analysis of those concerns which the students have made (different again), and then *show the students how an application of a particular process can help*

them work through a concern. The advantage of having a
clearly defined process is that it gives the students somewhere
to go with their concern—it does not open the kid up and then
leave him hanging as do so many attempts to "get at" kids. The
disadvantage of a precise process objective is the necessity to
make the process explicit and then join that neat little abstrac-
tion to a huge messy mass of concern.

The more explicit the process, the more helpful it is. There
are a number of ways to specify such processes. One of the simplest is to draw upon personal experience, by thinking back to
ways in which you yourself have worked out difficult problems,
and then generalize. In the academic fields, Jerome Bruner's
idea about "the structure of the disciplines" suggests a number
of processes which can be used to understand new material.
Similarly, psychologists can catalog a variety of different processes which people find useful in dealing with social or personal
changes. Works of literature, particularly autobiographies such
as those of Benjamin Franklin and Malcolm X, contain many
examples of men learning by insight and then applying that insight consciously to new situations. Finally, the students themselves are an excellent source of information about the kinds of
processes which they need, or already have and can teach others. These various sources might suggest such diverse possibilities as generating negative categories, hypothesizing, reducing
to single variables, reducing to first principles, second guessing,
backing into a corner, flipping out, and analyzing function.

Once the process is clearly identified and understood by the
students in an intellectual form and its meaning for them is analyzed and discussed, they should experiment with using it. *Experimentation with a new process should be done first in class,
where there is the support of the rest of the group for trying
out new behaviors, and then in as many different situations as
possible.* The more situations that students see a process can be
useful in, the more wholeheartedly they are likely to try it

themselves. Finally, if the student is going to utilize the process in real life, he will need to practice using it there. "Homework," in a process curriculum, is working on the process at home. Students should be encouraged to specify what applications of a process they want to make to their own lives. The class and the teacher can help to make sure that these applications are reasonable and can act as a support group later to check up on students, help them reassess results, etc. *Without specific goal setting, support, and follow-up, there is little likelihood of change.*

There is a variety of different forms in which the What, So What, Now What curriculum can be taught effectively:

I   the improvisational approach

American schools spend millions on educational materials —textbooks, language labs, teaching machines, computer consoles, science kits, and learning games. Much of it is junk; some of it is very exciting; all of it is expensive. But we ignore the one material that is never junky, that is always exciting, that is always there, costs nothing, and is more complex, sophisticated, responsive, and dynamic than any other. Our students are our best educational materials. Every classroom has thirty teaching machines. All they need is to be plugged into each other.

Many of the most effective methods of teaching process depend on using the classroom environment—the kids themselves —as the basic teaching material. *In such an improvised approach, the students' common concerns determine the process emphasized; examination of their diverse behavior is the basic teaching method.* For example, we have often used an exercise in which the students lock the fingers of their right hands together so that the thumbs are upright and free, as in the old thumb fighting game played by children. Then the students are asked to imagine that they are their thumbs and that their thumbs must meet their partners'. After performing such an exercise, the students can be asked to write haiku, or very short poems, about their experience. The following poems, the top row by second graders, the second row by fifth graders, and the last row by college students, suggest the kind of concerns that are revealed:

second grade

We played together
We looked eye to eye
He said hi to me.

I was ascared then
I was afraid of him then
He was not a friend.

fifth grade

We had a wild fight
and we trapped each other
    down
till we got tired.

We were talking with thumbs
It was very fun
We were almost finished
then we were done
And you know who did it
    with me?
        MISS RUBIN!

college

The fat scrunchy thumbs
hide, hello, hit, hug and hurt
just like little me's.

Fearfully watching
Active and playful frolics
I cannot respond.

If the teacher's interest is in literature or creative writing, there is obviously plenty of material here. If, however, the teacher's interest is in teaching something about the processing functions, then he may want to take the poem which seems to get the most general response from the class or the one which has most moved its author and follow that through the What, So What, Now What sequence. If he concentrates on the Sensing process, then a lesson might be laid out as follows:

PROCESS: SENSING OTHER PEOPLE

explanation of sequence

class activity

What

Immersion in a new experience of touching others

Students interlock fingers of right hand with thumbs free, and are told to imagine that they are their thumbs and that their thumbs express their personalities. They are to meet their partners and write poems about the experience.

Reorientation into someone else's way of relating.

Examine poems which show concern for relationship. What would it feel like to be the poet's thumb? The poet? What do the poems say about the processes people use to relate to each other?

So What

Analysis and reevaluation.

What difference do these patterns of relationship make? Why does the poet's thumb feel as it does? Is that good? Under what circumstances?

Contemplation of other possibilities.

Sit and daydream about thumbs for a few minutes. What associations do they have? What role do these associations have in this exercise?

Now What

Experimentation with other ways of behaving.

Experiment with new ways of meeting the same person's thumb. See how many ways you can develop. Change partners.

explanation of sequence	class activity
Reapplication and commitment to a personal way of living.	Do you enjoy any of these other patterns of behavior? Pick one (your original if you like) and try shaking hands the same way. Try talking the same way. After class, try acting the same way for a few minutes. If you like this new way of relating, practice it and live it.

This is a complex lesson, and it exemplifies many important considerations about the What, So What, Now What process. First, notice how *it picks up all of the concerns but emphasizes only one process.* There is no simple one-to-one relationship between concerns and process. The same exercise could have been used to relate the same concerns to processes within the Transforming or Acting area. For instance, to teach how different people take the same experience and Transform it differently, the students could be asked to repeat the exercise and the haiku writing as though they were someone else in the room and then define the difference in meaning. To teach about Acting processes, the students might be asked to discover how many different ways they could find to express the same emotion, first with just their thumbs and then freeing their interlocked fingers and using their entire hands.

An important ingredient of the lesson's power is that it involves all of the students at the same time. *Every student can participate,* rather than reading about how someone else felt or hearing how a classmate responded. *Participation is made easy because the lesson is a game.* It is not an unreal encounter, but it is not ordinary life either—the rules are clear and arbitrarily set, the stakes are low, and therefore the possibilities for experimentation are maximized.

The thumb exercise is a very immediate lesson, and that usually makes it an exciting one. *But the more immediate the*

lesson, the greater the student's right to voluntary withdrawal.
If a student does not want to participate, he should not be
made to, or made to feel uncomfortable, and certainly his grade
should not suffer. The teacher has no way of knowing what is
going on in his head, and unless there is the chance for a long
personal conversation, the student is better off being the judge
of the benefit he can receive from the lesson. In the last analysis, he is the final judge anyway. *Do not push.*

Not only are all the students directly involved in this lesson,
but every student puts a physical piece of himself on the line.
In a culture as verbal as ours, *when the body is involved, the
heart is also.* Most of us are very good at covering up ourselves
with a screen of words; often it is easier to understand ourselves
by "listening" to what we *do* rather than what we say. But precisely because the body is a relatively open source of information on how we process our environment and our own feelings,
it is very vulnerable to attack. Teachers must be sure not to demand so much body involvement that the students feel embarrassed. Thumbs are good in this respect; even junior high boys
and girls do not get too nervous at that kind of contact. (Substituting noses for thumbs would up the ante considerably.)

Particularly when physical expression is involved, it is wise to
remember that if the teacher feels uncomfortable, so will the
students. Students have very sensitive radar; they know a phony
in an instant, and will be uneasy, suspicious, and wary. The lesson will fail, and neither they nor the teacher will have gained
anything. Gain security by practicing on colleagues, but do not
practice at the expense of students, and *do not push yourself
beyond your own limits of comfort and competence.* Teach
from what you have experienced and understand, not to test
yourself or to fulfill your own needs.

A teacher's comfort and self-confidence go a long way toward
making students feel easy and willing to take some chances
with themselves. But in addition to being accepting and open
himself, the teacher can encourage the same attitude in the class.

When a student does something which is difficult for him personally, the teacher should recognize that, just as he would comment upon someone who worked out a difficult math problem. Since all human communication depends upon a degree of honesty and more direct communication depends upon increasing honesty, those students who speak their minds and hearts should be praised for their forthrightness, whether or not the teacher agrees with them. But if one student makes harsh remarks about another, it is wise to stop and examine the effects of those comments, for if they are allowed to continue unacknowledged, they will ruin any chance of personal and honest communication. *Recognition of courage, praise of honesty, acceptance of hostility—these will help build the classroom support that makes it easier to change.*

A process lesson should never be split so that the analysis is in a separate session from the experience, or the analysis will be cold, stale, and irrelevant. The thumb lesson can be handled in one hour, but it will be much more effective if a longer time is taken. The last section of the thumb-lesson plan (Now What) is particularly rushed. Insight may come in a flash, but change rarely does. *Take time to let growth take place.* Do not expect miracles or conversions, and do not try to produce them. Little changes, which are understood as they happen, grow in a geometric kind of ratio, like a savings account—the more, the more. As long as growth evolves slowly, there are likely to be few crises, and the lessons can be kept within an educational setting. The purpose of the process curriculum is to give students the ability to change themselves, not to work overnight wonders.

While the thumb lesson and the others outlined later should not produce crises, that does not mean that they will not cause pain to some students. Remember that *to be open to joy is to be open to grief.* Both are part of being alive, and the process curriculum is an attempt to help students be more alive more of the time. The student who writes in his haiku that he is

"Fearfully watching" but "cannot respond" is probably feeling pain. If he can be taught to respond, he may have less fear, and less pain in such a harmless interchange as the thumb game. But he cannot process the world or life selectively.

2   curriculum materials

The thumb game begins and ends with the student himself, leaving plenty of room for personal improvisation. Another approach is to start with an outside statement of concern and then work toward a process to meet it and ways of applying that process to personal action. Many works of art, literature, and music can serve as the general or metaphoric statement of concern, but as we discovered in the early summer programs, the teacher must then do a great deal of work to get these perspectives to make a difference in a student's own life. It is possible, however, to construct curriculum materials which give a general or metaphoric statement of concerns and also include a structure which will help the teacher open out new process understanding.

Monster Monster is one example of such material. It deals with the concern for control by letting the child advise someone who has lost control—a monster who does not want to be a monster. It is one of twenty beginning readers (The *My Books*) designed to combine reading exercises with stories that speak directly to students' concerns. Other books in the series use the physical activity of shaking hands to help students explore friendship, use breathing to develop a sense of personal rhythm, and use drawing to sketch a vision of future selves. In each, the text is extremely simple, and provides an opportunity for the child to use his new reading ability to find out about the issues of greatest importance to him. (See Appendix 3, page 202 for complete description.)

The pictures in *Monster Monster*, originally rendered in color, were drawn by my five-year-old son. Their childish qualities are meant to encourage other children to draw their own pictures. (If you have a young friend, get him to decorate your book for you. Be sure to ask him to use his own imagination and not to copy. A few questions about TV monsters, Halloween, and dreams will get him started.)

MONSTER
MONSTER

Story by Terry Borton
Pictures by Mark Borton

I AM A MONSTER.

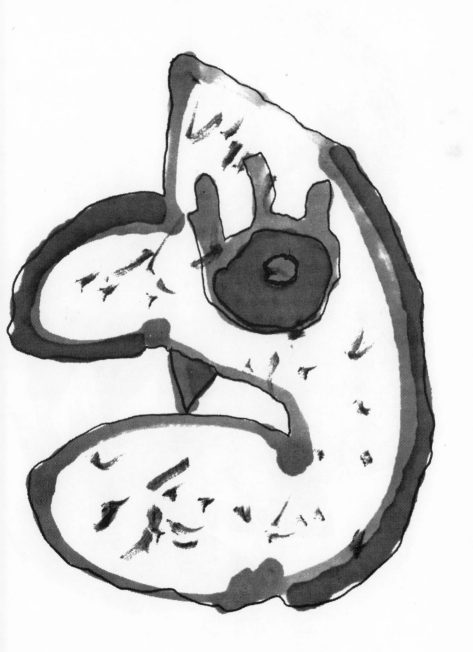

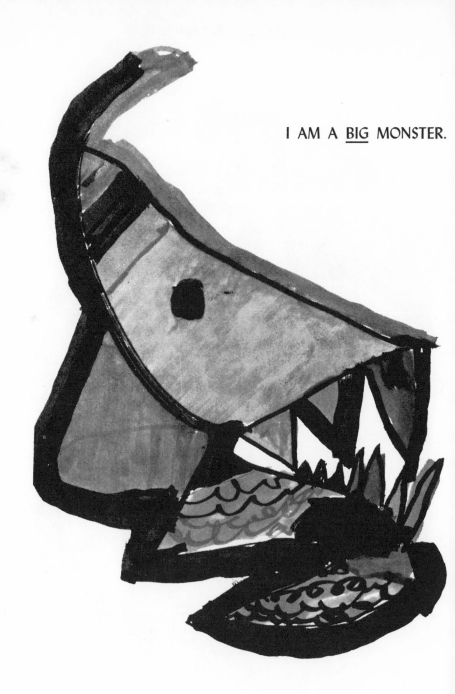

I AM A <u>BIG</u> MONSTER.

I AM A MONSTER MONSTER.

BUT I DON'T WANT TO BE A MONSTER MONSTER.

I DON'T WANT TO BE A MONSTER AT ALL.

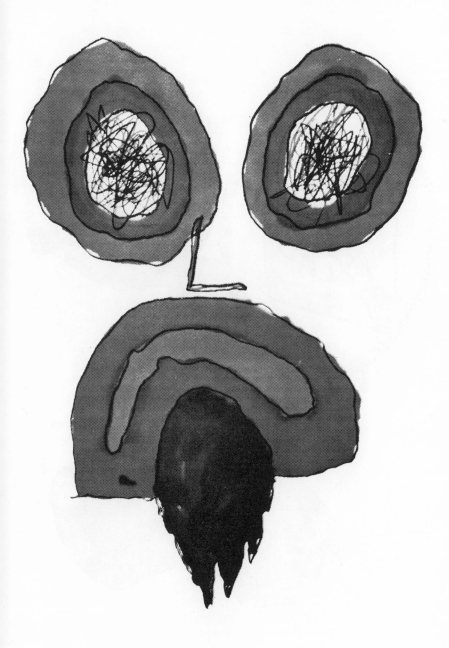

NOBODY LIKES A MONSTER.

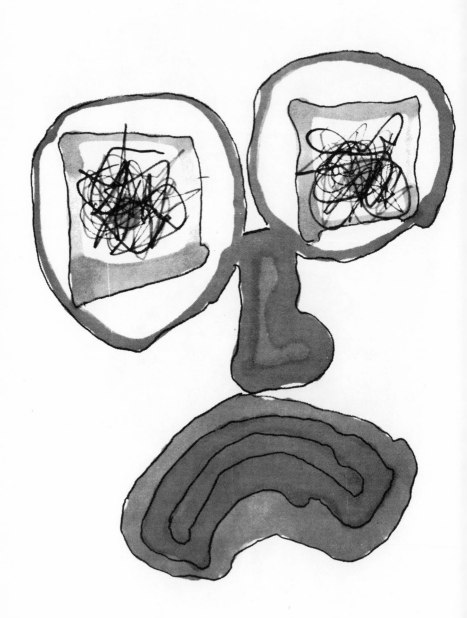

I WANT TO BE LIKED.

KIDS ARE LIKED.

I WANT TO BE A KID!

I WANT TO BE A KID LIKE YOU.

YOU ARE NOT A MONSTER ARE YOU?

I CAN BE AS SMALL AS A KID.

BUT THEN WHAT DO I DO?

The *Monster Monster* allows the child to follow someone else, the monster, through the process of conscious self-examination. But as the monster begins asking for the child's help, the two draw closer together. What begins as a book about the monster's problem ends with the child beginning to think about what makes a monster a monster and what difference there is between a monster and a man or between a monster and himself.

The *Monster Monster* lesson follows the What, So What, Now What sequence:

PROCESS: TRANSFORMING

explanation	book lines
What	
Immersion in the experience of being a monster, which in itself requires reorientation.	I AM A MONSTER. I AM A BIG MONSTER. I AM A MONSTER MON- STER.
So What	
Contemplation—has anyone heard of a monster who didn't want to be a monster?	BUT I DON'T WANT TO BE A MONSTER MON- STER. I DON'T WANT TO BE A MONSTER AT ALL.
The monster analyzes his state and compares his life with that of the child reading the book. The child becomes involved in the same process, particularly if a teacher encourages him to think about what the monster is saying.	NOBODY LIKES A MON- STER. I WANT TO BE LIKED. KIDS ARE LIKED. I WANT TO BE A KID! I WANT TO BE A KID LIKE YOU. YOU ARE NOT A MON- STER ARE YOU? NO! YOU ARE A KID.

explanation

Now What

The monster experiments with a new way of being. The child is now asked to choose for the monster another experiment in action which will make him more like a kid. In this process the kid is also beginning to analyze just what is human within himself and to start the What, So What, Now What process over again on a more personal basis. One excellent way to do this is to have the student make himself physically "look like a monster" and then slowly turn himself back into a kid, observing the changes as he relaxes his muscles and softens the lines of his face.

book lines

I CAN BE AS SMALL AS A KID.
BUT THEN WHAT DO I DO?
WHAT DO I DO TO BE A KID LIKE YOU?

One of the great advantages of books like *Monster Monster* is that they are indirect while still being explicit. That is, the focus of attention is not directly on the kid, but on the monster, yet the book deals with basic concerns of the young child in a very immediate way. *The more direct a lesson, the more threatening it may be. Take it easy.* A direct attack on concerns requires digging down into the child's soul in order to be effective, and that is not a job for a teacher. A process emphasis keeps the attention on the general processes which all people use, is much less threatening to the child, and is much easier for the teacher to handle.

Explicitness, or the degree to which basic questions are stated bluntly, is a matter of complexity, not threat. For instance, if a teacher repeatedly asked the three explicit questions of What, So What, and Now What, he would end up with a simpleminded curriculum which the kids would understandably ignore. It is the complexities these questions acquire when buried in human situations which gives them their power. Sometimes it is useful to have the questions asked in their boldest and most explicit form, but an *explicit answer to an explicit question can never encompass the complex and muddled truth.*

3   revamping old lessons

There have been some thirty or forty lessons mentioned in earlier sections of this book. Almost all of them succeeded in tapping the concerns of students, but many of them made the mistake of dealing with the concerns themselves; they failed to move from the concerns to an understanding of the process which met them and thus give the student power to change himself. Usually this mistake shows up because the lesson deals with What, So What, or Now What, but not all three. Once that fault is understood, however, most of these lessons have excellent potential. They are listed according to the process they touch and the parts of the What, So What, Now What sequence they complete successfully.

LESSONS

process: sensing	part of sequence successfully completed
Look at our school. What do you see?	What
Group writing of plays.	What, So What
Writing about pickled dog's head.	What, So What
Mirroring each other.	What
Concentrate on the city.	What
Nothing Personal, Miss Lonelyhearts.	What

process: sensing	part of sequence successfully completed
Pop poem.	So What
Street art rubbings.	What
Aria da Capo.	What, So What, Now What
Gibberish and Nazi indoctrination.	What, So What, Now What
See the city as a zoo.	What, So What

process: transforming	
Who are you?	What
Describe yourself ten years from now.	So What
Reverse racial identities and write play.	What
Paper on nightmare.	What
You look at us; we'll look at you.	What, So What, Now What
Who am I?	What, So What
"The Waking."	What
What is human about human beings?	What, So What
Animal herds, schools, packs versus human beings.	What, So What

process: acting	
Integration panel.	What, So What, Now What
Worm's-eye view of world.	What, So What
Beowulf versus Cassius Clay.	What, So What
Tug-of-war.	What, Now What
Explore space.	What
Make a cat out of space.	What, Now What
Nazi storm trooper.	What, So What, Now What
"Triumph of Will" and blindfold.	What, So What, Now What
Making cocoons.	What, Now What
Role playing of father and son.	What, So What, Now What

It is clear that most of these lessons were limited to What questions, without including the So What questions which might tie them to a broader understanding. Nor did they extend the process to a wider usefulness by asking Now What and experimenting with how it might be tied to personal action. Consistently, the part of the lesson which got the shortest shrift was Now What—the one which was most likely to make the lessons applicable to the student's own lives. And consistently, the lessons (such as the Nazi indoctrination, the "You look at us," and the integration panel) which did encompass all three processes were the most memorable lessons and those which "made the difference" in how students behaved afterwards.

Most of these lessons might be reworked to give a student a more complete understanding of a process related to his concern. For instance, the worm's-eye-view lesson can be expanded according to the What, So What, Now What model below:

PROCESS: ACTING

explanation of sequence

class activity

What

Immersion in new experience by reorienting the perspective.

Have class write about what it would be like to be a worm coming up in a city, on a drag strip, etc.

So What

Analysis of the meaning of physical and psychological perspective.

Discuss papers. Why do the worms see things as they do? What can they see that we can't?

explanation of sequence	class activity
Contemplation through imagination.	Sit for a few minutes and imagine that you are a worm. What is your life like? What do we mean when we say of someone that "he's nothing but a worm?" What would it feel like to be such a person? Would a giant lying down have a worm's-eye view?
Now What	
Reorienting and analysis by repeating the first phases in a more immediate setting.	Write about what a human worm would see in this school. How would things seem to him?
Experiment with personal behavior.	Spend a day pretending that you are a human worm. What difference does it make? What things can you do that you could not do before? What things are you not able to do?
Reapplication, choice, and recognition of consequences.	Go through the What, So What, Now What processes above for a human eagle. What is the difference between a human worm and a human eagle? How much choice do you have as to which you are going to be? Try behaving first as one and then as the other. Do your actions make you, or do you make your actions?

It is important, in lessons such as these, that students not be manipulated. By manipulation, I do not mean telling them what to do or giving them directions. In the worm's-eye-view lesson there are plenty of directions given, although there is also plenty of room for student direction, as in the case of my own student who wrote that magnificent paper on Holden Caulfield. *Manipulation is telling students one thing and meaning another.* Such dishonesty is often very tempting because it can seem to produce such powerful lessons. It would be possible, for instance, to treat students as worms—degrading them with contempt, ridicule, irrelevant assignments, and busywork. After such an experience of what it means to be a worm, the students should be able to write much more effectively. But because the students had been manipulated into the experience, and the teacher had contrived it without telling the students that it was contrived, they would be more likely to resent the lesson than to learn. The lesson the students would learn is that they must never trust the teacher because they could never know whether the teacher was simply playing a game with their emotions which would leave them feeling exposed and foolish. *All process teaching is built on trust;* if the students ever come to believe that their teacher is working on assumptions which are hidden from them, there will be no trust and little of the kind of learning the teacher wants to encourage.

Of all the mistakes which can be made in teaching to the concerns of students, manipulation is the most seductive. It is the mistake I have made most often myself (the Nazi lesson, for instance), and it is the one I most regret. Gradually I learned that if I told the students what I was going to do and why—told them, for instance, that we were going to role-play an invasion by Nazi storm troopers—I could get almost as much impact as through manipulation, without creating mistrust. In addition, the lesson could be conducted much more safely. If students think a contrived and manipulated situation is a real one, they will react as if it were real. If the situation is strange to them, they will have very little control over their behavior, reacting just as any of us would if we did not understand what was happening to us. They may behave in ways which would embarrass them or offend their classmates, or they may even become physically violent. If, however, the students know in the back of their minds that they are role-playing and that the situation is not real, they can always cut themselves off if things are getting out of hand. Role playing and improvisation are powerful techniques for experiencing what a given situation would be like. Once they are started, such improvisations create their own emotions and involve teacher and student equally. *Manipulating an illusion of reality perverts a teacher's power and a student's learning; intentionally simulating reality increases the options for both.*

4   sources of techniques

Additional examples of lessons which can be either used as they stand or easily developed to deal with process concerns are available in published form. For instance, *Learning to Work in Groups* by Matthew Miles describes the sensitivity-group techniques which may be used to work on the process of sensing. *The Productive Thinking Program* by Martin Covington et al. provides a process approach to problem-solving skills in the transforming area. And Viola Spolin's *Improvisation for the Theater* has been instrumental in our efforts to turn insight into action. Other appropriate works are listed in Appendix 3, page 201.

5   reach, touch, and teach

This entire book is an example of the What, So What, Now What sequence. The initial chapters were designed to immerse the reader in a new set of experiences so that he would be able to reorient his perceptions to see what I saw and feel what I felt. The middle sections, dealing with theory, consciously trans-

formed these experiences into a new model for teaching. This
chapter and the concluding sections provide examples which
may lead other teachers to create and define their own processes
and perhaps eventually to build a more human and more humane kind of education for our schools.

6 new process courses—communications and urban affairs

In the last two years, the Philadelphia Public Schools Office of
Affective Development, directed by Norman Newberg, has been
extending and deepening the work we began in the summer
program. The present plan of the office is to develop over a
three-year period a K–12 track in two districts in Philadelphia,
providing parents, students, and teachers with the opportunity
to choose a fundamentally different approach to education. At
present, the most advanced portion of this project consists of
two semester-long high school courses, one in communications
and one in urban affairs. The courses use a more sophisticated
version of the What, So What, Now What model discussed
here to specify particular processes within the broad categories
of Sensing, Transforming, and Acting and integrate them with
the more traditional subject matter of English and social studies. The communications course concentrates primarily on intra-
and interpersonal processes, while the urban affairs course (written by Henry Kopple) concentrates on social processes.*

The choice of processes taught, the way they are presented,
and the kinds of material chosen to illustrate them reflect our
own personalities and interests. Such an approach contains an
obvious danger of narrowness, which we have tried to avoid by
getting the advice of subject experts and other teachers. But it
also represents an important supplement to the usual method of
building curriculum by committee or by corporation. For us, a

* For further information, see Appendix 3, page 205. Related films now
available are described in Appendix 2, page 191.

piece of curriculum is a work of art, like a poem, a sculpture, or a happening, and at its best is a personal expression of what is best in us. Its impetus is our own search for insight into our lives and society. Its value as curriculum is determined by its power to reflect to others what is true about their world and about themselves.

forces in a new field

A new field is forming, and it needs a name. It can be defined —roughly—as a new direction in education, stemming from the cooperation of psychologists and educators and balancing the traditional emphasis on skills and cognitive information with an explicit attention to the important areas of feelings, values, and interpersonal behavior. Projects with these goals are sprouting up all over the country. Some, like ours, come from within the schools; others come from within the universities, the various branches of psychology, the arts, and business. Names for the field have grown up as fast as the projects: "psychological education," "affective," "humanistic," "personological," "eupsychian," "synoetic." Several of these terms are a bit bizarre, and none of them has yet become generally accepted. But their presence serves to indicate the increasing attempt to find a language, a philosophy, and a set of practices which will help schools teach those processes most directly related to human creativity, learning, and growth.

There are a number of ways to pursue that attempt. One is teaching experiences of the kind I have described in most of this book. But there are other approaches to the new field which can be equally productive and which can bring to education a wider perspective, a more formalized theoretical base, and new clinical expertise. The increased interest of psychologists in curriculum, classroom climate, and educational objectives is beginning to serve that function and is likely to have profound effects over the next several years, perhaps much more effect than did the giant curriculum centers which developed as a result of the post-Sputnik criticism of education. For the post-Sputnik curriculum reforms were essentially attempts to find better ways to teach the traditional disciplines of math, science, or social studies—often with the effect of moving the college curriculum into secondary or elementary school. The projects in the new field do not only operate with different techniques; they also begin to define and develop new curriculum subjects and a new school orientation toward practical and applied psychology. Many of them speak directly to the need for a more relevant educational process and offer the possibility of creating a profound change in American education.

There are many different traditions behind the psychological practice now impinging upon education, and each has theoretical proponents working in the new field, supplemented by the clinical or applied approaches. Each tends to concentrate on the area where its theory or experience is strongest—the behaviorists on basic patterns of behavior, the depth (or Freudian) tradition on patterns of motivation and value, the clinical tradition on the expression of feelings and the creation of sensitive interpersonal relations. And each, of course, has its own peculiar problems which grow out of the limits of its approach. Taken together, however, they provide a wealth of knowledge and technique with which to build a more humane educational system and a more human student.*

Increasingly, behaviorists have moved away from simply running additional experiments with rats or pigeons and have begun to tackle the much more muddled situations of real

---

* Materials relating to each of these projects will be found under the principal investigator's name in Appendix 3, page 199.

human life. Applying the principles they learned from studying animal behavior, they have tried to change human behavior by regulating the nature and schedules of rewards for particular kinds of responses. For instance, Professors Michael Orme and Richard Purnell of Harvard became interested in experimenting with systematic positive reinforcement of desirable student behavior to curb discipline problems. Their interest was aroused when one of their graduate students, Wendy Gollub, reported back from her teacher-training observations:

> *I entered a classroom in which eighteen children seemed to be devoting all their energies to massacring one another, destroying school equipment and breaking the sound barrier. They were not only oblivious to observers but did not even acknowledge the existence of their teacher. The teacher could not prevent the children from disassembling desks, tearing up classmates' papers, hurling books across the room, and running around the halls at will. I saw no evidence of friendship among the children. In fact, during one half-hour's observation each of the eighteen children was hit or kicked at least once, ten of the children being aggressors.*

Clearly this was a classroom in chaos, and Mrs. Gollub was frightened at the thought of trying to teach it on her first assignment. In collaboration with her professors she designed a more appealing curriculum and classroom setting and then set up a system of "positive reinforcement" in which all undesirable behaviors of the students were ignored and desired ones were reinforced. A major component of the reinforcement system was a "store" which held a variety of tangible rewards such as candy, puzzles, model planes, comics, and trips. The "prices" on the items were proportional to their educational relevance; lollipops and gum were 10 points, a trip to the zoo was 450. The children could earn these points by showing desired behavior in consonance with such rules as "Do your work," "Raise your hand when you want to talk," "Be on time," and "Follow the rules." (These rules were worked out between the teacher and the students. Further experimentation would be necessary to determine how effective positive reinforcement would be if the children were rewarded for following rules which were imposed on them or made no sense to them—if, in other words, positive reinforcement were used alone without involving the conscious participation of the students.)

Once the connection between rewards and the desired behaviors was specified, Mrs. Gollub began to teach, awarding points whenever a child raised his hand, arrived on time, etc. The professors, using a TV camera hidden in a closet, collected tapes of the children's responses for later analysis. The analysis consisted of taking samples of behavior, and getting "blind," or "naïve," raters to note "time on task," "frequency of disruptive behavior," and other measures of whether the kids' behavior was in consonance with the teacher's objectives. The advantage of this technique was that it could establish a very precise link between the teacher's behavior and the response of the students. In this case, the researcher could also check out the efficacy of an old behaviorist assumption that behavior could be controlled by using only positive rewards. Behaviorists usually say that while behavior can be shaped by punishment as well as reward, punishment is undesirable because of its possible bad side effects.

Accordingly, Mrs. Gollub did not punish the children for their bad behavior, but passed out points ("concrete reinforcements") at the rate of 20 to 100 per child a morning, plus a generous supply of "teacher reinforcements" such as verbal praise and physical hugging. Immediately the room began to change. Most of the children busily began to earn points, their eyes sparkling. But a few children rebelled:

Andrel shouted, "I don't want any more points; stop giving them to me!" Then he marched around the room boasting that he did not care about earning points. The other chil-

dren, still interested in points, ignored him completely. Soon,
he sneaked unnoticed to his seat where he began working fu-
riously to earn points again.

Mrs. Gollub did not punish Andrel for shouting and running
around. She simply rewarded the kids who were doing their
work and ignored Andrel, difficult as that was.

Focusing on desirable responses and ignoring undesirable
ones requires a desensitization to disruptive activities [on
the part of the teacher]. It is natural to notice a child danc-
ing rhythmically in the corner of the room, while overlooking
the child reading quietly at his desk, but readjusting these
perceptions gives phenomenal results, and demonstrates the
efficiency of positive reinforcement in shaping behavior.

From Mrs. Gollub's point of view, the experiment was a success
—it allowed her to teach. The researchers, after analyzing their
television tapes, were equally pleased. Though the experiment
had not gone on long enough to see if the kids' behavior could
be continued if they no longer received points, their "time on
task" for the experimental period had increased from about 50
percent to a fairly stable 80 percent. The researchers were somewhat uneasy about the "blatant sacrifices in precise experimental control" which working in a real classroom had involved,
but they concluded their study by saying that their kind of research might not only identify important variables for future
study but "lead to greater sophistication in the definition of
teaching techniques that work."

Just as the pressure for "techniques that work" has moved
the behaviorists from the laboratory to the classroom, so the in-
heritors of Freud's depth psychology have felt increasing pressure to apply academic theories to real social phenomena and
document the effect with statistical research. One of the most
extensive examples of an attempt to take Freud's insights and
put them into a quantifiable and applicable form is exemplified

by the work of David McClelland of Harvard's social relations department. McClelland began working on problems of measuring the motivation of rats deprived of food, then performed a series of experiments to measure hunger motivation in human beings, and then devised a system for measuring "achievement motivation" in man by counting the frequency of its appearance in fantasy images. He defined the need for achievement (n Ach) as a pattern of thought and fantasy about doing things well and discovered that those people who had such a pattern were characterized by a preference for moderate-risk goals, a desire for immediate feedback on their performance, and a liking for personal responsibility. McClelland reasoned that if a society had a great many such individuals, the society itself should show outstanding achievement, and he spent twenty years in a mammoth research effort to substantiate his claim that achievement research provided a "factual basis for evaluating theories that explain the rise and fall of civilizations." The next step was to devise educational methods for increasing the achievement motive in people who had little of it and to test out these methods in this country and abroad.

Dr. Alfred Alschuler, director of the Harvard Achievement Motivation Development Project which is one result of McClelland's research, is in charge of a federally funded five-year research project to assess what factors lead to effective achievement training. The project has devised many classroom techniques for increasing achievement motivation in students, most of them involving experiential learning which takes place in a game situation. I visited one training program for teachers and attended a session which used a contest in making paper airplanes to demonstrate to the teachers how achievement motivation affected their students.

There was a lot of joking around the table, as everyone felt a little nervous.

"Now they're going to use the old carrot on us," cracked a little physics teacher sitting on my right.

The head of a math department, an enormous man, smiled broadly, first at the physics teacher, and then at me. "Feeling cutthroat?" he asked.

I didn't say so, but I was, and he knew it. My "n Ach" was way up. We eyed each other while we set our own quotas for the number of planes we would make.

Dr. Alschuler gave us the start sign. I was making planes feverishly; out of the corner of my eye I could see the math-department head moving more slowly but doing a better job—the quality-control check at the end of the game might go in his favor. The physics teacher was using mass-production techniques, making one fold at a time.

At the end of five minutes the game was up, and we were all laughing at the tension it had produced. The physics teacher had more planes than any of us, but his mass-production assembly had failed—all the planes were missing one wing. I had the second largest number of planes, but several had sloppy folds and were disqualified.

"Nuts to this," said the physics teacher. "I'm not going to get another heart attack over a bunch of paper airplanes. Next time I'm dropping my quota in half. I'm only going to make six."

I was swearing at myself—I should have been more careful. The second time through the game I would set a slightly lower quota and do a better job.

The math teacher was smiling broadly. He had won.

Later we all talked about our experience in the game and how our own behavior did or did not reflect the characteristics of a high achiever. Did we set moderate-risk goals? Did we utilize information about our success and failure? And then we began to dig into the more fundamental value issues which were involved. Suppose that we could use games like the paper-plane competition to teach students the characteristics of a high achiever and through a variety of such exercises could actually train a student to think and act as one. Would that be a good thing? Did we want to subject our students to the pressure that we had felt? Could we decide that achievement training was good for some students who were not achieving up to our standards and bad for those who were too competitive? On what basis?

Just as researchers are becoming involved in the practical questions of education, so clinical psychotherapy is getting up off its couch and finding ways to add its skill to solving school problems. In San Diego, for instance, child psychologist Dr. Harold Bessell had joined educator Dr. Uvalo Palomares to set up the Human Development Training Institute (HDTI), which has now trained a thousand teachers in a primary school curriculum to improve a child's self-confidence, social interaction, and awareness of his feelings. The basic procedure is to have a group of children sit in a circle and talk with each other and the teacher in a semistructured way. At an HDTI training session which I visited, a teacher conducted her demonstration sessions with a group of primary children set up in front of 150 watching teachers. She began the second session by following the detailed instructions given for each lesson in the teacher's manual.

"Today we are going to have a chance to tell how something gives us a good feeling. This little doll makes me have a good feeling because I thought I had broken it, but a friend showed me how to fix it up again. That gives me a good feeling because I have had this doll for a long time, and I didn't want it to be broken. Now would one of you like to tell me something which gives you a good feeling?"

There was silence in the group. The kids shifted a little uncomfortably, as did we in the audience. Then Joyce put up her hand. We began to crane our necks for a better look. Joyce was a brain-damaged child who had sat huddled into herself on the previous day's session—chewing on a hangnail.

"I can ride my bike."

"You can ride your bike, Joyce! I bet that does give you a

good feeling. And you look so pretty when you say you feel good."

Joyce was sitting on her hands now, bouncing up and down, her little blond face aglow. The audience relaxed and glowed with her.

The game went on around the circle, each child getting a chance to express what it was that gave him a good feeling, and being praised by the teacher. The procedure was powerful, since the kids began to discover that some of the things they thought were unique to them were also shared by others—feeling good because a father was coming home from the war or because their friend liked them. And the procedure was simple—simple enough so that teachers could handle it effectively. But human beings, even very little ones, are not at all simple, and the tight structure of the HDTI program sometimes trapped the teacher. What kind of simple praise would be appropriate to give, for instance, to the little boy sitting beside Joyce who said that being able to sleep made him feel good because he knew his father had "insumnia"?

The simple and carefully programmed aspects of the HDTI program are in marked contrast to the eclectic approach of the project run by Dr. George Brown of the University of California at Santa Barbara. Brown's project, sponsored by the Ford Foundation through the ebullient Esalen Institute, utilizes many different approaches, but particularly the theories of gestalt therapy which attempt to get kids in touch with how they are feeling in the "here and now." With this theoretical orientation in their background, the teachers in Brown's project are encouraged to devise their own techniques to integrate affective and cognitive learning in order to achieve a "humanistic education."

I joined the teachers at one of the monthly meetings where they learn about new ideas and share with each other the techniques they have developed. Gloria Siemons, a pretty first-grade teacher from Goleta, California, was describing an exercise which she had first conducted with the entire class, and then used when one child became angry at another. She lined the class up in two rows on the playground and had them find a partner, put their hands up facing each other, and then push.

Push they did, laughing all over the field, especially at their teacher, who was being pushed around in a circle by several of the bigger kids.

Later, when two boys got into an argument at recess, Mrs. Siemons simply asked them, "Are you angry now? Would you like to push?"

"Yes I'm angry. I'm angry at him."

Both agreed to the contest, pushed for a minute as hard as they could, and then collapsed into each other's arms giggling. Their anger was worked out, but without hurting each other.

"What would happen," I asked Mrs. Siemons, "if one kid pushed another hard enough to hurt him?"

"We have a rule about that. 'It's OK to be angry with someone, and it's OK to push, but it's *not* OK to push him into the rosebush.' "

Good teachers, particularly good first-grade teachers such as Mrs. Siemons, have always responded to the affective, emotional side of their students' lives, and it is precisely this intuitive gift which Dr. Brown is capitalizing on. By systematizing such techniques and relating them to a general theoretical framework, he and the teachers on his staff have begun to generate hundreds of ways to integrate the feelings of students with the regular curriculum taught from kindergarten up through high school.

Interestingly enough, another group of psychologists and sociologists who are working on issues directly related to education have, until recently, had much more response from business than from educators. The National Training Laboratory (NTL) Institute for Applied Behavioral Science has been associated with the National Education Association for years but until the last few has devoted most of its energies to training business executives in major corporations and governmental organizations such as IBM, Standard Oil, and the State Department. NTL "trainers," all of whom are highly screened professionals, use the "laboratory" approach to teach people about their characteristic patterns of relating to others. The laboratory involves presentation of relevant theory and question-and-answer sessions, but the heart of it is the "T-group." ("T" for "training." Also called "sensitivity group" or "encounter group.") The T-group, which NTL pioneered in 1947, usually consists of about a dozen people who meet together for anywhere from three hours to several weeks, following no set agenda, but using the development of the group as a way of generating data about group behavior.

In the Summer Project of 1967, we used T-groups as a major portion of a teacher-training program which we ran for a junior high school. Students and teachers were mixed together on a first-name basis for the entire project, which began with a two-week T-group conducted by trainers from NTL and then moved into other courses and activities directly related to improving the teachers' regular school program. A selection from a "Dear Friends" bulletin of that summer describes what happened:

The purpose of the group was to encourage each individual to gain a greater insight into himself, an increased sensitivity to the feelings of others, and an awareness of how these two were interrelated. It differed from an ordinary working group in that it provided for maximum feedback of personal feelings. Most of us, most of the time, do not say what we feel, even if we pride ourselves on saying what we think. And yet the undercurrent of feelings often determines our behavior and the response of others to us. The training group provides a setting in which enough trust is created so that it is possible to find out what others feel about us. It is a bit like talking with a good friend, except that in the training group

*there are a number of people in which to mirror one's self,
and therefore a greater check on the accuracy of perceptions.
Obviously, such trust is not built up easily; in fact, the creation of it is one of the main issues on which the group
spends its time. And when people begin to talk about their
true feelings, the result can be either exhilarating or painful.
There was plenty of laughter and warm feeling during the
first two weeks; there were also tears. Teachers who had been
working together for years suddenly discovered that they
never understood each other; race came boiling out in unex-
pected places; teachers vied with each other to get the reti-
cent students to talk and winced to find that their habitual
way of relating to kids was to grill them. But most important
of all, a climate of much greater openness was created. It became legitimate to disagree in public, to show affection in
public, to raise questions about why a group leader, a department chairman, or a principal operated as he did.*

*The period after the T-group was devastating. We expected
it to be, but that did not make it much easier to live
through. The participants were removed from the warm security of the T-group and placed in new groups with classes
in drama, urban affairs, and professional management. The
attempt to make the honesty of the T-groups work in a situation where trust had not been built slowly created enormous
tension, and classes dragged through a series of hot murky
days.*

*Gradually, however, the mood changed as new kinds of rela-
tionships were established and people found that it was possible to operate in more normal situations and still apply
many of the values of the T-group. A group of the teachers
interviewed parents whose children had transferred out of
school. They began to get excited about changing the conditions which caused these transfers, and organized a new reading program for the school, a staff development program*

*using T-groups, a special program for problem students, and
a host of smaller projects. As they got further into these programs, the issues—of scheduling, of personnel, of power, and
of authority—became very close and very hot. With the
hope of actually doing something in their school, pressure to
move fast and cut corners created violent arguments. Some
members of the group threatened to walk out, for instance,
when the group's leaders submitted a proposal to the administration which had not been approved by the entire body.
But these complications, which would probably have killed
the proposal two months ago, are being faced now, as members of the group find ways to make even their anger a constructive force.*

In retrospect, the T-group was clearly the most successful
part of the program, though the teachers continued to have
trouble putting their experience into practice, particularly back
in school during the winter. For the students in the groups, the
sessions were not so successful—the adults tended to monopo-
lize the conversation, and the groups were just too talky. Very
little work had been done using such groups with students,
and at the minute there seem to be few rules of thumb to go
by. Our own experience, both in the teacher-student project
and since then, suggests that T-groups can be vey helpful in
clarifying concerns and feelings *if* they are handled by a compe-
tent trainer, are kept short, and are carefully worked into a
larger program which teaches processes to handle the concerns
being revealed.

Though the programs and projects I have described here are
a good cross section of the new field, they are by no means all
that could be discussed. There are hundreds of different techniques and dozens of theories and programs. But though they
differ in many important respects, they have a number of features in common with each other and with our own work.

First and most important, all of these projects teach in a very

explicit and direct way to the student's feelings, behavior, interpersonal relations, and values. It is the fact that they are so explicit and direct which sets them apart from most of what has
traditionally been "school." Schools have usually concentrated
on the subject content of math, science, and English and have
ignored or actively suppressed feelings. The new programs make
what was covert into the subject of overt discussion; they make
the implicit explicit. They make feelings legitimate, they clarify
them for the students, and they suggest a variety of behaviors
which he can use to express them. They do so on the assumption that if these feelings (or concerns) exert a powerful effect
on a student's behavior in the present and will do so in the
future, it makes sense to deal directly with the major sources of
that behavior, not just with the binomial theorem, the gerund,
or the Seventeenth Amendment.

Second, many of the projects encourage what Dr. Alschuler
calls "a constructive dialogue with one's own fantasy life." In
the case of n Ach training, this means encouraging students to
fantasize about doing things exceptionally well, and then helping
them tie dreams to reality by carefully planning goals. In addition, many of the projects encourage students to talk about
their dreams, both night dreams and daydreams, and help find
ways to make them useful. At its simplest level, this means talking about the personal things that give a child a "good feeling";
at a more complex level, it means (as in one of our lessons)
sorting out his own personal visions of heaven and hell; at a
deeper level, it means (as with some of the Brown project exercises) acting out the characters in a dream. Again, the assumption is that dreams are an important part of human experience;
that though they are very personal, they are not "bad"; and that
there are legitimate and useful ways of sharing them with others and with one's self.

A factor of the new programs which often causes misunder-
standing is that most of them emphasize nonverbal experiences,
either through physical expression and involvement or through

art, sculpture, or music. For the most part, this concentration upon the *non*verbal is not *anti*verbal or *anti*-intellectual. Nonverbal educational techniques are based on the obvious but little-utilized fact that a child learns most of his emotional-response patterns at a very young age—before he can talk. His knowledge of love, rejection, anger, and hunger does not come through words, but through his sense of touch, of swelling in his throat, of gnawing in his stomach. Even later, when he begins to talk, the words he learns are "Mama," "doggie," "see"—words for things and actions, not feelings. Indeed, many children seem entirely unable to give a name to their current feelings—they have been taught how to say "I am bad," but not "I feel bad." Education which deals with feelings is often facilitated by skipping over the verbal labels which have been learned relatively late in life, regaining the other senses, and then reintegrating them with verbal thought and new behaviors.

Another common technique which causes confusion is the reliance of many of the programs upon games, dramatic improvisations, and role plays. Again, though those utilizing the techniques believe in fun and use games, few of them are simply advocating "fun and games." Their interest stems from an insight into the learning process of small children. By playing games—house, fireman, office—the small child learns what it will be like to be an adult and begins to develop his own style in that role. But our culture provides few such opportunities for older children or adolescents, even though the society is changing so fast that many of the response patterns they learned as three-year-olds may be no longer relevant, and may even be dangerous. Games and improvisations allow a simulation of the self. While they are real and produce real emotions, their tightly defined limits provide a way to try out new behavior without taking the full consequences which might occur if the same action were performed in ordinary relationships.

Games, nonverbal interaction, fantasy, a more explicit attention to feelings, values, and behavior—these are the ingredients of the new field. It is developing because educators and psychologists are working together to find ways to teach students about the processes which will be central to them as persons. It is important work. For, as Dr. Mark Shedd, superintendent of schools in Philadelphia, said in an address to a mass meeting of teachers there, "It is the passion and the power of humanity that we seek to expand when we teach reading or math or any other school subject. If we divorce school work from the guts and hopes of human beings, we should not be surprised that our students find school gutless, hopeless, and inhuman."

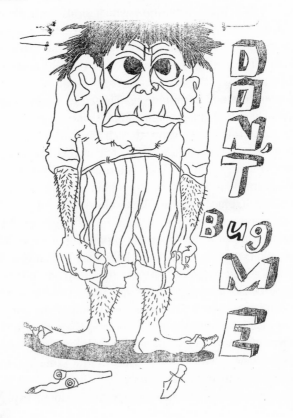

disciplined concern

The gutless, hopeless, and inhuman school denies life, and it is difficult for lifeless students to learn or to be free. But attention to the processes which relate to students' immediate lives does not inevitably mean a rampage of "student freedom"—though unfortunately the two are often lumped together.

Ever since I began teaching in experimental programs, the confusion between relevance and freedom has plagued me. The first summer the school's administration worried about whether the students would have to wear shoes, the second summer they worried about long hair, the third about smoking, the fourth about classroom noise. Each time we tried to handle the issue in a way that seemed reasonable—sometimes defending the students, sometimes not. People occasionally got very upset, but somehow all the excitement seemed beside the point. Though our students were generally quite free, we were not primarily interested in giving them more freedom, and resented having to spend so much time debating the point.

Yet freedom was the issue then, and still is. In some cities, they cane students into submission; in many places, they slap, shake, and shove them. In many more, teachers subdue kids with threats, sarcasm, insults, innuendo, and ridicule. Like beat-

151

ings with a blackjack, these techniques crush but leave no marks the eye can see.

I think kids should have more freedom than they commonly have in American schools, much more. I certainly do not want to defend teachers who use unreasonable punishment to control their classes. But I have come to feel that it is a major mistake to equate educational relevance with greater liberty for students.

The freedom-authority continuum ought not to be the only line along which battles for educational innovation are fought. There will be battles there, of course, and given the nature of American society, they will be spectacular ones. But they should be thought of as the rear-guard action of experimental education. Otherwise we will find ourselves fighting for student freedom only because we know that the old educational system has failed and hope that our students can do better on their own. The championship of freedom would then become no more than an admission that we have nothing relevant to teach.

The confusion between freedom and relevance takes its heaviest toll on the new progressive teachers—bright young people who care about kids, and who want to find educational methods more suited to their needs. They are open to innovation, but they assume that innovation means letting a student do what he wants to do. Reacting to tales of harsh discipline, they are horrified if a child is spanked at school, though they probably spank their own children at home. In suburban schools their "freedom classes" work—depending heavily on the students' "proper" upbringing or a continuous computerized check of their whereabouts, as in the Meadowbrook School in Newton, Massachusetts. In the tough urban schools, the new progressives go through hell.

The older teachers who have learned to tongue-lash look at these beginners and say, "You can't control a class." "You don't have the guts to stand up to the kids."

That is not the problem. It is not particularly difficult, after all, to look mean for the first six weeks or to learn the razor intonations used in dressing down a class. The problem is that the irrelevant curriculum, which is so obviously failing in the big cities, is closely associated with rigid and harsh discipline. The problem is that relevance has been equated with freedom and discipline with punishment. The problem is the kids.

Bob—a senior in my slow section. On my first day of teaching he took the seat directly in front of my desk and interrupted my introductory remarks by asking, "You new?" When I nodded my head, he grinned, "We got your number." From then on he made my life miserable, always quitting just before I got to the breaking point. A month later he was suspended by some other teacher; a month after that he was jailed. At about the same time I learned that he had started as a freshman in the best academic class, and had been moved down one track each year as various teachers retaliated for his wisecracks.

Joyce—a pretty, bright, and pleasant cheerleader who would *not* stop talking. Her rah-rah mentality plus her incessant chatter irritated me to such a point that I found myself hating her. But one day she was absolutely quiet. I was describing *Johnny Got His Gun,* a book about a soldier who loses his legs, arms, eyes, ears, nose, and mouth—yet still lives, and spends twenty years thinking about his condition. Suddenly Joyce ran from the room crying. I didn't know what to do—finally I left the class and found her sobbing on the staircase to the attic. Her older brother had been completely paralyzed from birth and was beginning to develop violent convulsions.

Tom—a very short hoodlum who sauntered into my class looking for trouble. When he discovered that I was not out to "get him," he started to write. Not assignments—never assignments—but complicated pornographic poems loaded with religious imagery. Two weeks later his girl friend sulked into one of my other classes—a beautiful girl who wore an ornate gold cross dangling between heavy breasts. A month later Tom was suspended for failing all his courses except mine, and a few days later his girl friend was suspended after I broke up a fight in which she ripped the clothes off a rival.

No teacher could get to know students like these—not typical students perhaps, but not so unusual either—without realizing that their classroom behavior is meshed in the complexities of human lives, often tragic lives. Badgered by authority, terrified by family crisis, torn between sex, love, and anger, these students seem beyond petty injunctions to arrive on time to class. Particularly if their teachers come from a background where passions are covered with pleasantness, the raw openness of emotion has a power which nothing in the arid atmosphere of school can match. The harshest of teacher threats is mild compared with what the students already suffer; the final school penalty, expulsion, is a pitiful parody of their rejected lives.

And so the teacher, feeling compassion for his students, puts up with an untenable and unteachable situation. He cajoles and exhorts. (I counted one teacher telling a class to "Be quiet" thirty-four times in one period.) Or he makes rules which he carefully outlines for the class and then breaks because he knows what is behind some boy's action. Or he breaks his heart trying to make such fascinating lessons that all his students will be involved and then finds—as he half knew he would—that the room is in such chaos that no one is involved.

It is an impossible situation, and one that I have sweated out myself more times that I would care to admit. I have no easy answers, but there are some general principles which have helped me keep a sense of proportion:

1 The kids have to be in school—that is the law at present.
2 As long as kids have to be in school, they ought—at a minimum—to find the experience profitable.
3 Preferably school will also be enjoyable and important.
4 School will not be profitable, enjoyable, or important if the kids hack around all day.
5 School is worthless unless teachers have something to teach.
6 If teachers believe that they have something important to teach and if they are going to try to teach it within the framework of compulsory education, then they owe it to

themselves and the kids to maintain the kind of order in which they can function.

I believe that there are important things to teach—facts, logical processes, psychological processes. I also believe that there are many different limits to the order which makes teaching possible. There is no simple correlation between the limits on freedom and the importance, relevance, or joy of the learning. Yet so widespread is the confusion between freedom and relevance that it is difficult to find people from whom to learn the distinction.

I met such a man—luckily for me—at one of the low points of my teaching career, a two-week substituting job in Philadelphia. I was an utter failure as a substitute. The easygoing teaching style that had served me well with the classes of Bob, Joyce, and Tom collapsed when faced with a substitute's necessity to command instant and continuing order. When I asked for help, the principal sent me to watch one of her "best disciplinarians," George Straus. She told me he was "traditional," and so he turned out to be. I did not learn anything new about a more relevant curriculum from him. But I was reminded that good traditional teachers—like some I had in school—do reach student concerns, and are more limited by the kind of curriculum they use than by the degree of freedom they allow.

George Straus turned out to be a young white teacher (the school was all Negro) with clean-cut features and a boyish face. His roomful of students was dead quiet, though I recognized some of the morning's troublemakers. Straus was starting a slide-tape lesson on France, and was trying to get a slide projector to work. He got it unjammed, but then the tape recorder broke down. I watched for the kids to react, but there was not a movement. This guy must be an incredible tyrant, I thought—those kids are petrified.

Finally all the apparatus worked, and France was presented in a series of slides and the voice of Maurice Chevalier. It seemed like pretty dismal stuff to me, but the kids sat quietly enough. The filmstrip was over, the lights went up, and Straus asked his first question. How was life in France different from theirs?

A dozen hands shot up. One hand was chosen, and its owner spouted a whole list of comparisons. Another hand added more. Hands in the back disagreed. Debate surged back and forth, but with one person speaking at a time, carefully, tightly disciplined. Yet there was a tremendous freedom of intellectual and social debate. Straus served as a wandering moderator, moving up and down the aisles, touching one student, then another. When the bell rang, the students were annoyed, but on signal rose one row at a time and walked quietly out the door to the bedlam in the halls.

I was impressed. I had seen very few teachers who had that kind of control and at the same time gave the personal warmth and intellectual freedom which I think are essential for students to grow. I was so impressed that I arranged to visit Straus on the first day of school the next year to see how he went about setting up his class.

A year later, a few more girls were wearing the "natural" or African haircuts, and open-mesh stockings were certainly new and in style, but the old noise and confusion in the halls was very much the same. Straus was standing at the door, finger to his lips, letting seventh graders into his room one at a time, girls to one side, boys to another. When the bell rang, Straus began by asking for responses to the first day of school.

There was a long quiet. "Uh, Mr. Straus."

"Yes?"

"I done lost my roster card." Everyone laughed.

"Well, you stop by my desk on the way out, and we'll fix up a new one for you. But one thing. After this, please don't call out. If you do, you will have to come in after school. We have only one way of being recognized here—with a hand. And don't worry, there will be time to get to each of you."

Then Straus began exploring space. Suppose everyone had left earth except Joan. (He was already good on the names.) Would Joan need any kind of laws?

"Nah. She be the only one."

"Wouldn't be nobody but her to follow it."

"Even if she broke it, she wouldn't bother nobody."

Slowly the group explored the reasons for rules and then began to make up rules for the class. One girl did not see why they had to line up in the hall for class. Straus agreed with her. He liked people who wanted to control themselves and was glad that she thought they could come into class without being made to line up first.

Toward the end of the conversation, when all the basic rules had been established, a heavy-looking boy who was slouched in the back row beside me straightened up and raised his hand. He wanted to shift chairs; he said his desk was too small. Straus talked sympathy. He said he understood how awkward it might be to adjust to tab arms after big desks in elementary school. And he talked promises—there might be new desks after Christmas. The boy was slagged back in his chair again. And then Straus told him that he could move, and that he had done exactly the right thing by asking instead of just moving when he felt like it. There was a triumphant grin on the boy's face when he moved, and I could feel the class relax. This rule-making game was actually going to pay off.

Straus was creating an incredibly tight system, all right ("It's the little things that make or break you"), but whereas many teachers set up such channels to say no, Straus was setting them up so that the kids could learn. The system worked because Straus stuck to it and because the kids could see that following it got results.

I am not unduly concerned that Straus controlled more of his students' behavior than I think necessary. His system was tight, but he used it to give students the option to think and speak freely and with dignity about themselves, their relation to

French culture, and a wide variety of other academic subjects. I am sure he could have used the same system to teach many of the lessons I have outlined earlier in this book. For once having established an order within which he was comfortable, he could tell the kids to enjoy themselves during an exercise like the thumb game, and they would understand the limits for their behavior, just as they understood why and how they were free to come into his room without lining up.

The essential point in maintaining an order which is consonant with a curriculum of concerns is not the particular limits set on behavior—whether kids sit with hands folded or whether they play thumb games. The essential point is *how* those limits are set and the *process* that is employed. I was particularly struck by this fact when I realized that—in spite of their obvious differences—Straus's class was very similar to the program of a young street worker named Bill Parr, director of the San Antonio Youth Project in Oakland, California. Rattling around in an old VW bus which serves as the transportation system for three hundred delinquent boys in the East Oakland area, Parr runs a freewheeling "relational therapy" session in the car. Parolees and probationers hail him on the street as he drives over the area making house calls, checking up on one of his boys who has cut school, or getting some kid out of jail. His boys are a far cry from Straus's decorous class. Their language is uproarious; they smoke constantly, wear do-rags around their heads (though Parr disapproves), and keep the bus in a constant tumult of shouting, laughing conversation.

Yet Parr is on excellent terms with the police, the probation system, and the schools, even though he has no official status and until recently was supporting the Project primarily out of his own pocket. The respect with which he is treated is due to the results he gets. The "return-to-jail" rate for his group is much lower than that of the official state agencies dealing with the same kids.

Though Parr's program seems at first to be totally undisciplined and unstructured, it has very strict rules which stake out the limits of behavior. Parr gets most of his boys out of jail, and in order to get out, they must promise to obey the law (no drugs, drinking, stealing cars, etc.) and to attend the Project's three weekly meetings. On these two points Parr is firm—if a boy does not comply, Parr will have him locked up again.

When Parr takes a kid out of jail, his environment has usually overcome him. An alcoholic father, a prostitute mother, a hostile school, friends on dope, the ever-prowling cops—whatever the particular combination, it has landed him in a situation where he is totally unable to handle himself and where no one he knows can help. He must depend on Parr.

"In the beginning," Parr says, "I do a lot for them. They become dependent like the children they are, and I make sure they're aware of it." He described, for instance, a jailed kid who tried to bluster past Project rules by bragging about what a big man his father was in the rackets.

"Will your father get you out of jail?" Parr countered.

Tough medicine, but the truth. And at the other extreme, another kid was whining that he did not want to get out of jail. "Nobody cares about me. My mother, my father, they couldn't care less. It don't make no difference to me if I sit here and rot. Who'd care?"

"Look," said Parr. "It's three in the morning. Why do you think I'm sitting in this jail if nobody cares?"

Once the dependency is established, Parr is able to create a personal relationship of trust based on the fact that he is a meaningful person in the kid's life—first the one who got him out of jail, later the one who keeps him out. And then he begins to demand more.

The discipline of Parr's program is in forcing his boys to face their chaotic environment—the alcoholic fathers, the prostitute mothers, the fights, the runaway girls, the temptations of pot and wine. "It's their reality," says Parr, "and they've got to find a way to meet it. Stealing a car and running to Mexico doesn't solve the problem. When they get out of jail and come back home, reality has only gotten worse."

And so Parr prods the motley-looking crew jammed into the VW bus to face their reality and talk about why they do what they do. The day I rode in the bus reality was a small boy's toe. He had no shoes, and his nails had become ingrown from wearing his little brother's boots. His big toe had become so inflamed that ugly red streaks were running up his ankle. The VW was making the rounds of the bureaucracy trying to get the necessary papers signed so that the doctors would operate on a public ward. But Juan was doing his best to run away. "No one going to pull off my toenail" was all he said, over and over. As we drove from the parole officer to the supervisor to the judge to the doctor to the supervisor to the hospital, the other boys worked on him. They were sympathetic and joking at first. Juan would not listen. Then they began telling grisly stories of their own experiences. Juan flinched, but still was not going to see the doctor. Then they opened up on him. They pictured the alternatives: Let things go by, hope the toe would cure itself "when you know it won't," watch the red streaks climb up to the groin, have the whole leg amputated. Or see the doctor. Juan was finally convinced. When the forms were eventually signed, he hobbled into the doctor's office by himself while his teachers watched proudly, sucking hard on their cigarettes.

They were harsh disciplinarians, those boys. The only life they knew was harsh, brutally and irrevocably harsh, like the paralyzed brother who haunted Joyce, the authority that broke Bob from the top of his class, the tortured love of Tom and his girl. In Parr's VW bus and in evening meetings they spelled out their code for each other against the particular crisis of the minute. Their discipline was in facing the things that faced them. Sometimes shouting at each other, sometimes crying, they fought out the alternatives they could make from their lives.

Parr's program was certainly much more relevant to the lives of his students than was Straus's class or any of my own classes. For all practical purposes it *was* their lives; just as the Synanon drug rehabilitation center does, it demanded the total involvement of its members. Clearly such programs can have a much greater effect on student concerns than can one which restricts itself to the classroom. (One good way to increase the relevance of education would be simply to get more of it out of school and into the community.)

But whether educational programs are conducted in a class or in a bus, the problems of control are the same, and it is the similarity of the methods used by Parr and Straus which impresses me.

At the most simple level, both Parr and Straus intuitively employ many of the techniques of behavior modification which Mrs. Gollub used with the class studied with the television cameras, though Parr and Straus use punishment, while Mrs. Gollub ignored undesirable behavior.

1   They specify the behaviors they do not want—speaking out of turn, stealing cars.
2   They specify the behaviors they do want—permission before moving, submission to medical care.
3   They punish the behaviors they do not want with a clearly defined set of punishments—staying after school, jail.
4   They reward the behaviors they do want with clearly understood rewards—moving a seat, a cured toe.
5   They "shape" behavior a little bit at a time—"After this, please don't call out"; "In the beginning I do a lot for them."
6   Above all, they maintain a tough-minded consistency. They mean what they say, and they make that plain from the very first encounter—Straus with his finger to his lips, Parr countering, "Will your father get you out of jail?"

A clearly specified, consistent, and incremental relation between behaviors and rewards—that is the essence of behavior modification. Straus and Parr employ it with expert skill. But they also move considerably beyond a behaviorist model, employing the concepts of conscious feedback and an improvised form of the What, So What, Now What model to help students set their own behavior goals and consciously work toward them.

Both Straus and Parr begin by helping the kid look hard at What is going on. What does it mean to have to go to school? What behavior is necessary? What does it mean to have an infected toe? What behavior is necessary? Then they dig into the So Whats, the conflicts of intention and purpose. Why are rules necessary? Why is it that running to Mexico will not work? Finally they begin to look at the Now Whats—at new behaviors to change the environment. Now what do you do to get a seat changed? What do you do to take care of an infected toe?

Both Straus and Parr believe they have something to teach, and the strength of that belief has led them to make discipline a part of their "curriculum." Both concentrate on making the kids see the connection between their own actions and what happens to them. By building this conscious awareness, bit by bit, they increase each kid's ability to look at his own behavior, evaluate it, and generate new options for himself. Because he is helped to understand what is involved, he gradually exerts more conscious control and becomes more able to take responsibility for the consequences of his own actions. By themselves, the kids had neither discipline nor control and were hopelessly at the mercy of the forces around them. Straus and Parr, in their very different circumstances, found a way to use "discipline problems" to teach the students processes which would meet their concern for power and control by creating new alternatives for them.

A relevant curriculum generates alternatives for students, and alternatives are a prerequisite for freedom. Sometimes the teacher can provide those alternatives by simply giving the student freedom from artificial restraint—much of progressive education and discovery curriculum has this as a main objective. But real freedom involves the students' ability to choose the alternative they want rather than accept the one they are driven to. That is the concept of freedom which should be the goal of educators, yet a teacher cannot "give" it to his students. They must win it for themselves. The best a teacher can do is to teach them the processes which will increase their ability to step aside from their own way of experiencing—to wonder at it, to question it, and to modify it.

flying high
and holding steady

—"You go to a great school not so much for knowledge as for arts and habits."
—"I tell the world of Charles, Because He a victim of circustance."
—"Maybe all that is really wrong is that I have a bad case of growing pains."
—"The only thing that is right is that the boys go into the boys bathroom, and the girls go into the girls bathroom."
—"I was late but I still say that I am not guilt."
—"Now I have a future, in ten years I will have a past."

I began by asking what they added up to—that combination of nineteenth-century educational philosophy and scruffy student papers; the whirling mass of kids, teachers, books; the love, the laughter, the riots, and the futility. I do not pretend to have the answer. But I think the experiences recounted in this book clearly point out a direction and the reasons for taking it. I hope that they also suggest some concrete steps (the What, So What, Now What curriculum model, the sample lessons, the materials listed in the Appendixes) which others can take to explore that direction for themselves.

The edge of any art is likely to be precipitous. Explorers at the joint edge of education and psychology must be doubly wary, prepared either to fly high or to hold steady. For much of this book I have been flying high—scouting the possibilities for creating saner schools where students are more open about their feelings, more careful in their thinking, and more responsible for their actions. But there are many problems, and overcoming them will mean holding a steady course, planning carefully, and testing rigorously.

First is the problem of determining what effects these educational programs have. As a teacher that was not a hard question to answer—I knew when I had a good class and when I had a bad class, when the kids were turned on and when they were turned off, when they were learning something and when they were drifting. I had enough information to feel justified in deciding what to do with my own classes, and later with experimental summer programs. But the larger the number of students involved, the more pressure to produce research evidence which goes beyond personal testimonial and exciting stories.

The Achievement Motivation Development Project run by Dr. Alschuler has an extensive research program, and his experience has made him feel strongly about the need for additional evidence before program expansion:

> *We have very little hard evidence that programs in this new field accomplish much more than natural maturation. We have claims, promises, and fascinating anecdotes. But we should not institute these programs in mass compulsory education without first using the most sophisticated research techniques we have to improve them and explore their consequences.*

Dr. Alschuler's warning is well taken, yet on the other side is the tremendous pressure to do something to change those current educational practices which are having such overwhelmingly negative consequences. The teacher, principal, or superintendent cannot afford to wait until all the evidence is in; he must somehow balance the strength of his knowledge against the necessities of the situation and make a decision about what he is going to do. One way to help in that balancing process is to suggest a variety of ways in which programs from the new field could fit into the schools.

1   turning kids on

The easiest way to employ these methods is use them to get kids involved in the regular school program. Indeed, this is how I myself became involved—by using improvisations to teach *Huck Finn* and poetic dreams to teach *Lord of the Flies*. Now there are thousands of new techniques (see Appendix 3, page 199) which could be used to teach English, or the isosceles triangle, or the coding of DNA. They would add life and excitement to the study of any subject now being taught.

2   bits and pieces

In addition to using the techniques as "motivators" for the standard subjects, schools may want to experiment with small, self-contained curriculum pieces. Units such as are represented in Appendix 3 range from those which deal entirely with personal growth, to those which use a process approach to integrate personal and academic learning. Some are very short and can be used as a single lesson or a week's unit. Others provide the material for a semester's or year's work. Offering such materials in elective courses is a good way to try them without necessitating total commitment. An even better testing ground is a summer program, for there a more comprehensive range of courses can be offered, and much of the "schoolishness" of school is absent.

There are some problems with the bits-and-pieces approach —most of them stemming from possible contradictions with the regular program. Many of these can be avoided by a little foresight in planning so that a noisy drama class is not next to the school's grammarian. Given such elementary consideration, a new course ought not to disrupt the regular program of the school any more than does gym, advanced placement, or shop. Of course, if the teachers get excited, if the students want to learn, if one or both want more, then a more comprehensive approach should be considered.

3   the three-tiered school

Schools currently allow students to choose a "general," "vocational," "commercial," or "academic" track. If a larger investment in the new curriculum is desired, a special track might be constructed which gives it special emphasis. A more formal extension of the same idea is the three-tiered school described by Fantini and Weinstein in *Making Urban Schools Work*. One tier would be devoted to the acquisition of skills and knowledge such as reading, computation, writing, social studies, sciences, and other disciplines. The second tier would provide the child with the opportunity to explore his own particular talents—play a tuba, write a play, do individual research. The third tier would be devoted to the kind of personal and social objectives discussed in this book. Different teachers might handle different tiers, and much of the curriculum would be conducted on an individualized basis or out in the community.

4   a new curriculum

Though it may not develop within the foreseeable future, it is still worthwhile to speculate about what might happen if we made a clean sweep of the present curriculum and began using process principles to integrate skills, training, subject matter, and the students' personal and social concerns. Of course such an enterprise would require an enormous amount of time and money. The usual cost for developing a new course such as the recent ones in physics or social studies is about a million dollars and three years of extensive cooperation between scholars, teachers, and assorted experts. Building a new kindergarten-through-twelfth-grade program which required reorganizing all subject areas would be a mammoth job even if the will and the way were present. And at the moment, not even the knowledge for a general outline is available.

But it may be. The first prerequisite would be to answer (in process terms) that old question "What are schools for?" Clearly the answer cannot be that students should know any particular content, for the sheer amount of knowledge available to learn is already doubling every ten years. Soon many children will not be able to get even an elementary introduction into important fields. (Many do not even now.) But we should be able to identify basic *processes*, both logical and psychological, which every child should know and be able to apply on his own.

The identification of these processes is one of the major tasks ahead. I have already suggested the sources of help in such an enterprise—subject specialists, psychologists, literature and auto-biographies, artists, teachers, parents, and students. The list of processes will be an enormous one, even for the elementary grades. Students should know *how* (not what)—how to use a syllogism, coordinate three variables, see themselves from some-one else's point of view, fantasize at will, perform systems analy-sis, read precisely and at high speeds, generate a range of actions to express degrees of any emotion, etc., etc. Some processes will sound familiar; some will not. But each should specify what we want the child to be able *to do* by the end of an educational ex-perience.

Once having specified the objectives in process terms, we will need to determine what processes should be taught at what age in order to be most useful in meeting the concerns students might have at particular times. The rationale for the selection of processes can be built by teaching various processes at different grade levels and picking the level at which the students seem the most responsive. This empirical approach can be buttressed with knowledge gained from such developmental theories as those of Erikson in psychosexual development, Piaget in cognitive development, and Kohlberg in moral development. Perhaps it will then be possible to teach students the processes they want to learn when they want to learn them, so that students will learn and understand much more.

Of course students would not graduate from such a curriculum knowing what they now know. But neither would they *not* know many of the things that they now do not know—either in subject content or in process areas. For most of the important content which is now taught would continue to be taught—except that it would be chosen because it taught particular processes to meet student concerns. For instance, suppose that a school decided that one of the things it wanted a child to be able to do was to speak two languages. If it taught the second language when a child is most concerned with gaining control of his world through the process of symbolic manipulation—at ages three and four—the school might discover that one year of a bilingual pre-school was equal to four years of drudgery in a high school language lab. In junior high school, when students are bursting unevenly into puberty, schools might easily meet their students' concern for sexual relationships by offering classes which range from the present "plumbing courses" to those indicating the influence of sex in the development of world history. In high school, when students are concerned about the new identity which will be forced upon them by approaching occupations, the processes involved in role theory might be taught so that students would have a better understanding of the pressures about to be placed upon them and the ways in which they could use these pressures to help themselves grow according to their own devices.

Such a curriculum would suggest fundamental changes in school organization and administration. Precisely what changes is difficult to forecast, but a curriculum which emphasizes processes rather than mastery of content should make the teacher more a guide than an oracle; a curriculum which recognizes feelings and emphasizes honest communication should democratize a school and give parents, teachers, and students a greater say in its operation; a curriculum utilizing individual diversity should have quite a different grading structure, and might well abandon grades in many areas.

These changes may occur anyway because of the pressure of the knowledge explosion, community control, teacher power, and student power. The schools are a part of the changing society which supports them, and change within education will depend heavily on changes in the outside world. But if schools devote themselves to a curriculum aimed at teaching the processes of growth, students should enter that world able to change it, as well as to change with it.

No matter what form the new curriculum takes and no matter what place it finds for itself in the school, it is clearly going to raise a variety of immediate political, ethical, and public policy problems.

Politically, programs with both the potential and the liabilities of these are obvious hot potatoes. It is unclear as yet how projects designed by psychologists will fit in with current efforts toward more community control and what seems to be the resulting concentration on "teaching the basics." Even a mode of politics which is in consonance with the ideals and methods of the new programs is unclear, for the vision they present is often as utopian as that in George Leonard's book *Education and Ecstasy*. How to get from here to utopia without waiting until 2001 is a complex political problem. Suppose, for instance, that a school district decided to adopt an entirely new curriculum and school organization based on the concepts I have been discussing. What then would be done with the kind of bitter teachers Jonathan Kozol describes? Fire them? What of their feelings, their concerns, the painful history behind the collapse of those who have spent years trying to cope with a situation they could not understand or control? Teachers will surely declare that they are as human as the children, and they have the unions to back them.

The most fundamental problem, and the one which is likely to get people the most upset, is the ethical question caused by changing the expectations of what schools are for. At present students go to school to "learn stuff," and though they may expect schools to provide information, they do not expect schools to change them in any fundamental way, or even to offer that opportunity. Schools *do* change them of course. But many of the actual forces molding student personalities—the forces of authority, expectation, triviality, and tedium documented by Fredrick Weisman's film *High School*—are never acknowledged by the schools. They are smothered under pious clichés about building character, teaching good citizenship, maintaining high standards, and upholding human dignity. If schools ever begin to take these clichés seriously, spell out exactly how they are going to achieve them, and then do it, the public will suddenly become very concerned with ethical issues. They will begin to ask good, tough questions about what twelve years of a given kind of schooling does to a child. Unfortunately, their attention will probably focus on the new programs which are clear and explicit about their objectives, rather than the traditional programs whose goals can be fuzzy because they are only for show. But educators should welcome such an opportunity for serious discussion about what should be taught, how it should be taught, and what the expected outcomes and implications are.

If, for instance, everyone agrees that all children should be motivated, should they also be "achievement motivated"? At what age? Who decides? And who teaches? What will be the line between therapist and teacher? What is to stop teachers from working out of their own needs rather than for those of their pupils? Should teachers who share an important confidence have the same legal privilege which a lawyer or a minister has? How can parents and children be assured of the privacy which is their right?

The progress of curriculum that deals with student concerns and the resolution of the political and ethical questions it raises will depend in large part on the kind of teachers who become involved. What kind of people should these be? Our experience so far gives us some rough ideas, but they are very rough indeed. We have not been able to predict with much accuracy who was going to be a good teacher in our programs and who was not. A number of times teachers who seemed to understand what we were talking about and seemed eager to try out the new materials turned out to be unsuccessful over the long haul. Others who were "up tight," resistant, awkward, or openly antagonistic, turned out to be very successful in the classroom.

Still, there are some rough guidelines. First of all, the successful teacher has had previous experience. New teachers in any field have their hands full—they have not yet learned to make the rigmarole of school second nature so that they do not pay attention to it and can concentrate on the kids. If they have to handle an entirely new curriculum at the same time they are learning how to survive in school, they are likely to be in trouble.

The successful teacher is likely to have placed more emphasis on the kids than on his subject, no matter what that subject may have been. His first concern is that the kids understand the subject—not that they spout it back to him in the same pristine form that he spouted it back at his college teachers. If his first interest is in people, then he will move toward a curriculum which speaks more directly to their concerns, and will not be overly worried about whether it is the same curriculum he has taught before.

A crucial characteristic of the successful teacher in the new field is that he have the honesty to see what is there in front of him and the courage to act on what he sees. This will mean that he knows what the kids in his classes are doing, knows what is happening inside himself, and is constantly trying to make the two connect. He will be the kind of person who is willing to experiment with new material and with himself—not just at an intellectual level but at a personal level as well. Having always been involved in change, he will not be afraid of a philosophy which says that change is the business of education.

The training which such a teacher needs in order to handle the new curriculum is not difficut to arrange. First, he should have experience with the ideas and techniques at a personal level—he should participate in a T-group, take an improvisational drama course, try out exercises such as the thumb game with his peers—in short, put himself through more intensive and extensive experiences of the same kind that his students will have. (See Appendix 3, page 199, for sources of training.) Then he must be given an adequate supply of materials and techniques so that he will not suddenly be caught with "nothing to do." (One of our early mistakes in teacher training was to presume that we could "turn teachers on" and then expect them to generate their own new material. Very few people can do that while carrying a full teacher's load.) Finally, the teacher must be given tremendous support both in the form of backup personnel to help when he gets into problems and in the form of comfort if his efforts fail.

"Failure" is a loaded word, particularly in this field. If a math teacher fails to teach a good math lesson, then he fails to teach a good math lesson and just resolves to do better next time. No one, not even himself, would conclude that he were any less a good man, though repeated failure might raise a question about his skill as a mathematician or a teacher. But if the same teacher says that his goal is "to make students more human and more humane," then the failure of repeated lessons suggests that not only his teaching ability and subject competence are in question, but somehow his humanity as well.

No teacher, myself included, can operate under that kind of pressure. Certainly, if there is not a substantial connection between what the teacher professes and the way he behaves, there is cause to worry. But even if goals such as "making students more humane" are spelled out in precise processes, the teacher cannot be expected to use them all consistently or to be "expertly human." He cannot be judged by whether he can do the equivalent of square roots. But he can be asked to use his knowledge on himself and to be concerned about his own growth.

Often in the development of a teacher in the new programs there comes a point when he realizes that he is teaching something which could be useful to his personal development. For myself, this point came at the end of the 1966 summer program, when, on the last day of the summer, it became evident that neither I nor the other members of the staff were using the principles we were trying to instill in our students. Once we realized the discrepancy, we began putting ourselves through our own curriculum. We helped each other to look honestly at our personal interactions; to integrate our bodies, our emotions, and our thinking; to seek the processes which personally worked for us. As new people have entered the program, I have noticed the same turning point in them. It is as though we teachers have become so accustomed to teaching irrelevant curricula that we can hardly believe it is possible to teach material which actually could make a difference—not only to our students' lives but also to our own. Once that realization comes, once a teacher is growing because of his own efforts, and once he knows where he has come from and knows how he is changing, he will not feel the onus of being "expertly human." His own willingness to grow and his ability to help himself will serve as the same example for his students that the math teacher's expert knowledge provides for his young mathematicians.

But who, besides himself, is to teach the teacher? Where is he to get help? In part he can get help from those who have been over the same ground themselves and can point out the information and experience he will need. In part he can get it from his family—those who are closest to him, who care about him, and who will take the time to be there when he wants them. And in part he needs to rely on his friends and colleagues —the fellow teachers who share his principal, his PTA, and his coffee room and on whom he depends for support and for feedback on the observed effect of his behavior. Without such support and such feedback, change is not likely to take place. Again, to cite my own experience, it was not until my colleagues knew the issues I was working on that I got the understanding and encouragement, as well as the prodding, which made change possible. Their caring—its generosity and its quality—provided the room to grow.

Unfortunately, because of the way our schools are arranged, colleagues rarely have a chance to help teachers learn in the classroom. Colleagues can provide a climate that nurtures growth in teaching, but the cues on teaching itself are likely to come from the students. Again and again, as I look back on my own teaching, I am struck by how much my students taught me about their own needs. It was they who first said that the purpose of their education should be to know themselves and others "below the surface"; it was their fable of "The Toad" which pointed out the need to teach processes for handling concerns. Often I did not fully understand what they were saying until several years later, and I suspect that the things I said to them did not take hold immediately either. They could not "learn me" any more than I could "learn them." Each of us learned by himself, in his own way and in his own time. Yet we each listened, and we each changed.

I am convinced that students will continue to teach their teachers and that teachers will continue to teach their students. We will teach each other. We have different gifts to give, but we share the need to reach out toward what we do not understand, and touch what is still unknown.

student responses

The Berkeley High School
1967 Summer Project

Director: Jay Manley
Teachers: Anne Hornbacher
Peter Kleinbard
Montford Cardwell
Elizabeth Janssen
Barbara Glasser
Photography: Peter Kleinbard

In the summer of 1967, Jay Manley, an old friend who taught in Berkeley, California, and Anne Hornbacher and Peter Kleinbard, who worked in the first Friends' Summer Workshop in Philadelphia, joined Elizabeth Janssen and Montford Cardwell of Berkeley to set up a summer program based on many of the Workshop's assumptions about students and learning. There was an extremely diverse student body and an attempt to use the diversity as part of the educational process; there was a morning program of drama, communication, art, and dance; an afternoon program when the students were free to set up their own projects; an informal atmosphere, flexible schedule, and cooperative planning among the teachers.

Perhaps the most important similarity between the Philadelphia and the Berkeley projects, however, was the emphasis on exploring basic questions about self-worth, relationship with other people, and ways to control one's own destiny. The students' response to this emphasis, as reflected in comments from a taped interview after the program and in pictures taken by Peter Kleinbard,* demonstrates both what students can learn

* Extracted from the full evaluation report of the Berkeley Summer Projects available from Berkeley High School, Berkeley, California.

177

under such conditions and what they have to teach about the purposes and conduct of education. The program has now become a part of the regular school year, operating as a "house" within Berkeley High School, broadening its scope to include history, science, and physical education, and extending itself out into the community.

In regular school the time you think the class is most together is when they're sitting there hating the teacher all at once. But in the Project there was an entirely different feeling. The class felt responsible for what happened in the class. And that's what I really remember.

You sit in your regular classes and no one gets to know the other people. I mean they're just The Other People. Wouldn't you like to walk up to the teacher and say, "Who Are you?"? I wish I could do that.

Usually I would sit in regular classes, think my own thoughts, and not care what anyone else thought. I never said anything, anything at all. But this year I have been. I think it is simply because of the atmosphere of the Summer Project, especially Communications. There I felt more sure of myself. Now, for me, it's more important—not to be heard, or to force people to believe what I believe—but to put forth a different kind of a view, my own. So far I haven't said anything just for the sake of argument. I've been talking out. In fact, I've been made leader of a little group in History. Anyone who knew me last year would hardly believe me because I never said anything. I'd just sit there.

Friday, in my regular English class, the same class I felt stifled in, it just happened that that day the teacher told us something about himself and some of the people who weren't talking before started talking. Maybe it will be different Monday because I got a very different feeling in that class than in previous classes.

And then she said something about going to the zoo. And really
I couldn't believe her. She was saying to really sit down for half
an hour and really watch those animals, and do all these specific things, and say hi to three people and all this. I was very
intrigued that she was doing this different, interesting thing.
And then I began listening to her, and that started it. Before
then, it wasn't anything.

In each one of the classes in the Project, I found that I was trying. Trying can't always be good. Finally it became: relax; stop trying and listen. Really listen. And look. And that seemed to relax everyone. In relaxing you watch other people, and also watch your thinking. And enjoy it more.

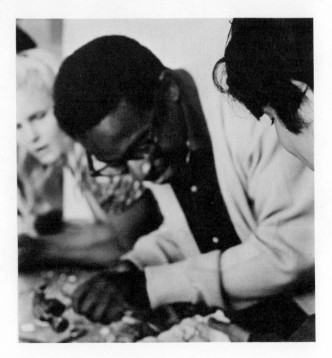

It has changed my attitude toward people and made impossible relationships possible.

Who Am I? Too complex a question. I find it even harder to answer now than six weeks ago. I think I said it before: I'm a person, a separate entity trying to retain separateness and yet to find union with another—I'm like everyone else for this is their struggle too.

In this project, we discuss what's on our mind and what's happening around us. We feel and touch where people seem to be afraid in regular school.

. . . and I was thinking about the interdependency of the two things because you have to have a sense of selfworth before you can have relationships with other people. And it seemed to me that the Project was a beautiful chance to develop these two things interdependently. And sort of help you in this way.

But now, after the Project, I have to stop and say, "Hey, isn't there something in this hall?". Then you really look and there is something there . . . I remember the first time I walked into Communications this summer, walking in and saying, "Yeech, this old hag." And that was kind of my first reaction when I walked into English this fall. And like, EGAD, here came the Project and it slapped me in the face and said, "Uh, huh . . . Wait. Sit down and think. And find something out. See if this teacher does have something to offer." And so it's getting better. All the time.

It's made me feel that my life is what I want to make it, and relationships with other people are also what I want to make them . . . What do I value? A person's right to be himself and not be inhibited by what other people want.

I have a different feeling inside that is hard to say . . . Everything is changed. I even talk differently. I make more sense. I really have learned to clarify and I have strongly felt the feeling of group responsibility, and of leading or starting a group. And I think this will carry on to school and that will be good.

It has made me a happier person with a new goal in mind: "To realize people are real." Teachers are real, my classmates are real, but most important: I'm real.

I'm a being in another living being called a world.
I may be small but I do exist.
I am a living soul with feelings as others are.
I am a machine as others are.
I am alive as others are and I am unique as others are.

LIFE

Some men think life is a fact.
It is something that just will be.
They spend it slowly, but unobjectingly.
They sit their life out with no regrets,
No unfilled dream they wish they could finish.
But I, I cannot do that.
I must live my life
I must cherish my life
For life is the ultimate blessing
And I shall not waste it.
For I will do, while others sit.
I will act while others wait.
I will fulfill my dreams
and my dreams will be of fulfilling.

I feel more spongy, like I have a new interest in things: ballet, opera, art galleries, 15 million wonderful ways—there's a door opening somewhere in me, I can feel the key in the lock now.

I can't say that I learned how to draw, or how to sculpt, or anything like that. But I can say that I learned, I guess, ultimately, throughout the project, that things are flexible.

Right now I feel daring, unafraid to do what I can towards being the person I'm capable of being. Less afraid to fail to be that person.

films

In our summers of experimentation in the Philadelphia Cooperative Schools Programs, we made movies to describe what we were doing, explain why it was important, and show how it looked. The films form a sequence, beginning with the introductory *Prelude* in 1966. In 1967 we produced four films, one on teacher training and one on each of the courses in communication, drama, and urban affairs. The films can be shown separately, but taken together they present a comprehensive and exciting introduction to the idea of a curriculum designed to teach processes which meet the concerns of students.

ALL FILMS ARE AVAILABLE FOR LOAN FROM:
Division of Instructional Materials
Audio-Visual Office, Room 328
Board of Public Education
Parkway, South of Twenty-first Street
Philadelphia, Pa. 19103
215-448-3315

Please specify a first and second choice of showing dates and requesting organization. There is no loan charge.

191

ALL FILMS ARE AVAILABLE FOR PURCHASE
FROM:
Film Makers of Philadelphia, Inc.
1729 Sampson Street
Philadelphia, Pa. 19103
Prices represent printing cost, including reel, can, and shipping
case. There is a ten percent reduction for orders of five or more
films.

Prelude $55
A Lot of Undoing To Do $71
Making Sense $47
Build Yourself a City $65
It's between the Lines $65

Prelude
A fifteen-minute, black-and-white,
sound, 16-millimeter film on the 1966
Philadelphia Cooperative Schools Program

Film makers: Oliver Nuse and Jim
Morrow
Script: Terry Borton
Music: Mike Merchant

Prelude was well named, for its content turned out to be just
as much a prelude for the staff as for the students. It is a strong
and delicate film which speaks in the language of emotion
about the educational possibility which the summer program
suggested and about the problems that the students sometimes
saw more clearly than did the staff.

The film begins with a student reciting a fable he wrote
about a toad who left his regular school swamp, found freedom

and acceptance in the summer school, and was killed when he returned to his old swamp. The narrator, speaking for the staff of the program, tries to show how the project was designed to prevent such an outcome. He explains how the classes operated and how the free afternoon sessions encouraged students to apply what they had learned to the real world. But the final section of the movie, in which the narration shifts to student poems, shows that while the students have a much deeper sense of themselves—of their pain, their loneliness, their beauty and dignity—they have little sense that they can make it in the outside world.

Prelude is not likely to change minds—the setting (a private school) is too idyllic, the assumptions behind the classes and student activities too implicit, the cinematic presentation too impressionistic. It is meant as the glimpse of a vision, a beginning which raises hopes and questions.

A Lot of Undoing to Do

A fifteen-minute, black-and-white, sound, 16-millimeter film about the teacher-student project of the 1967 Philadelphia Cooperative Schools Program.

Film maker: Jim Morrow
Script: Terry Borton
Music: Mike Merchant

A Lot of Undoing to Do is a hard-hitting film which describes an attempt to train teachers in the general philosophy of a process curriculum and then encourage them to generate the specifics themselves. The film begins in the project school, a ghetto junior high with all of the problems that has come to suggest. The grim atmosphere of the school affects both students and teachers in the same way—the movie draws striking parallels that show how both shut out the confusion, sleep it out, or tune it out. But the camera also picks up the bubbling energy of the students and the way they express their basic concerns for sex, power, identity, and relationship as they clown before the camera.

The jump to the summer training program is sharp, for here the students are on an even basis with the teachers—all of them involved in learning situations which include sensitivity groups, improvisational drama, and urban affairs. Together they talk in the sensitivity groups about how their personalities are affecting each other; they wander around the school blindfolded to get a new sense of their relation to their environment; they role-play a chaotic meeting to stop a riot; they argue out the procedural and philosophical basis for new lunch lines and guidance programs.

Back in their home school the teachers faced the tough problems of making their ideas work in the real situation. They had some success, but much of their enthusiasm was frustrated by the complexity of the problems, inadequate support, and a lack of knowledge about what to substitute for the current curriculum.

The final section of the film places this one summer program for twenty teachers in the context of the Philadelphia system's twelve thousand teachers, many of whom are struggling to find ways to change and cope with the enormous problems they face. Though there have been dramatic changes in Philadelphia's top administrative echelon, the movie makes it clear that change cannot come from the top alone and that an educational revolution will depend on teachers organizing themselves to meet the concerns of their students. The urgency of this need is dramatized through a powerful closing montage comparing the summer activity with current social upheavals.

A Lot of Undoing to Do is a film that rewards several viewings. Images of a desperate school, a chance for change, and contemporary violence are so compressed that important specifics are easily lost in the initial jolt.

Making Sense: Inside and Out There
A ten-minute, black-and-white, sound, 16-millimeter film on the communications course of the 1967 Philadelphia Cooperative Schools Program.

Film maker: Jim Morrow
Script: Norman Newberg
Music: Michael Merchant

Making Sense gives a brief glimpse into the way the 1967 communications course combined a multimedia approach with a series of metaphors to teach basic communication skills and understanding. The film shows how communication depends upon a reciprocal process—the message sent depending heavily on the message received. To make the communication process work, students use many different kinds of media—clay, writing, art, dance, film, photography, radio—picking the one which best suits their needs.

Making Sense follows the students through a series of analogies which helps them understand the many facets of communication. In "man as animal" students go to the zoo to examine the difference between animal and human communication. In "man as player of games" they study the way games can allow new communication because the rules are clear enough to make new behavior safe. In "man as a dreamer" students explore the possibilities of touching the pre-logical, symbolic, and emotional roots of communication. And in "man as player of roles" the students use the many voices heard on the radio to study how social role affects what and how information is transmitted.

When we filmed *Making Sense,* we were not teaching particular processes, but the film gives a good example of how a process curriculum moves back and forth between hard confrontation or analysis of a subject and a more encompassing, contemplative approach which allows the time and the quiet for personal growth. This combination of confrontation and contemplation grew out of attempts the year before to vary the amount of tension the students experienced. The new phraseology made the process much more manageable, and the fluctuation between the two modes of engaging the world became a basic flow which we later incorporated into all our courses.

Build Yourself a City
A fifteen-minute, black-and-white, sound, 16-millimeter film on the urban affairs course of the 1967 Philadelphia Cooperative Schools Program.

Film maker: Oliver Nuse
Script: Henry Kopple, Norman Newberg, Donald Bruce

The narration of *Build Yourself a City* uses an argument from three different perspectives to explore the 1967 urban affairs course. One viewpoint represented is that of a curriculum developer; the second is that of a traditional social studies teacher; the third is that of a ghetto resident who helped teach the course.

As the course unfolds, the students study the racial, social, transportation, and housing patterns of the city, as well as the promise offered by the richness and diversity of many cultures concentrated in a single area. They visit the police center and argue with the police representatives; they ride on a single trolley from suburbia to slum; they sit through a legislative session.

Finally they become involved in the question of urban re-newal—should slums be demolished, the people moved out, and new houses built where the old stood? The students decided that a better solution to housing problems would be to build low-income housing out in the suburbs and break up the patterns of segregation. They presented a petition to the mayor, organized a picket, and presented their ideas before the city in a letter to the editor.

As the movie progresses, the argument between the teachers jumps back and forth from the students on the screen to the educational questions their activity raises. What should be taught —ancient history or modern sociology? How should it be taught—through books or through trips, interviews, and debate? Why should it be taught—because there is a body of knowledge students should know or because students should be trained in the knowledge and forms of expression they will need if they are to "build themselves a city"?

The closing section of the film puts the course in the context of the urban realities in which the students are growing up. Riot, the voice of last resort, is a common occurrence for them. The urban affairs course presents an alternative to crises becoming the form of change.

It's between the Lines: Drama for the Classroom
A fifteen-minute, black-and-white, sound, 16-millimeter film on the drama course of the 1967 Philadelphia Cooperative Schools Program.

Film maker: Oliver Nuse
Script: Norman Newberg
Music: Peter Connor
Richard Hogan

It's between the Lines explores the 1967 course in both improvisational and formal drama. As the movie cuts from one class lesson to another, an improvised narration re-creates the kind of instruction which the students on the screen might be receiving. The effect is one of easy, rough-hewn informality which both describes the rationale behind the course and gives a sense of what actual sessions sound like.

The lessons concentrate heavily on the body and the ways it can be used to express feeling and meaning. The students, mostly of middle school age, practice finding the limits of their own bodies, building a man from junk and making themselves into musical instruments or the animals they have seen on a zoo trip. In later exercises they explore the space in their schoolroom as they first explored themselves—moving the chairs into mazes through which they climb and into fantastic constructions which they transform into organic moving machines.

A striking sequence follows an improvisation based on studies which show that rats kill off members who leave the pack and attempt to return. After working through the improvisation as rats, the students developed a scene taken from Shirley Jackson's "The Lottery," in which a group of human beings singles out one person to be marked for death. The closing image is an unforgettable lesson on scapegoating and how close animal and human experience can be.

The kind of sustained concentration exhibited by the improvisations shown in *It's between the Lines* proved invaluable as a technique in teaching conscious understanding of psychological processes. The following year, therefore, we ceased teaching the drama course as a separate entity and wove the approaches and philosophy into the courses in communication and urban affairs.

resources

It is helpful for teachers to have had some experience in exploring their own feelings before working with students on a feeling level. There are many groups set up for this purpose, but teachers should take care in choosing one to join. Groups which are not affiliated with some organization should be avoided, and the personal, professional, or experiential qualifications of the leader should be examined carefully. More and more schools of education are offering courses in "group process" or "sensitivity groups" or "humanistic psychology" or "affective education" where good training can be had under careful supervision. The National Training Laboratory, an associate of the National Education Association, 1201 Sixteenth Street, N.W., Washington, D.C., conducts training sessions for all levels of school personnel. In addition, there are a number of "growth centers," or informal institutes where experienced leaders conduct short-term training sessions. A list of these centers and of colleges offering training can be obtained from the American Association of Humanistic Psychology, 584 Page Street, San Francisco, Calif.

There are a number of books, movies, and exercises which are a useful introduction to new materials that recognize feelings in the classroom and try explicitly to encourage personal growth. This bibliography is only suggestive. A much more extensive bibliography compiled by myself and Dr. Alfred Alschuler is contained in the first entry below. For books on process education, see note, page 76.

Alschuler, Alfred (ed.), "New Directions in Psychological Education," *Educational Opportunities Forum*, New York State Department of Education, Albany, N.Y., June, 1969. To be published as a single volume by Education Ventures, Inc., Middletown, Conn. A collection of articles dealing with various approaches to psychological education in the schools. Topics covered are strength training for teachers, achievement training, process courses, solo experiences, value clarification, creativity training, sensitivity training, etc. A bibliography of 300 items is included.

American Association for Supervision and Curriculum Development, 1201 Sixteenth Street, Washington, D.C. 1966 Yearbook, *Learning and Mental Health in the School*, and 1962 Yearbook, *Perceiving, Behaving, Becoming*. Both books contain overview articles which represent the increasing interest among professional education groups in the mental health and personal growth of the student in school. *Life Skills*, the 1969 Yearbook, discusses the development of process education in both academic and personal areas.

Jones, Richard M., *Fantasy and Feeling in Education*, New York University Press, New York, 1968. Discusses the relationship of the humanistic-education emphasis on fantasy and feeling to such major curriculum innovations as the Educational Development Center's "Man: A Course of Study." Criticizes Jerome

Bruner's theory of instruction and attempts to make distinctions between psychotherapy and education.

Miles, Mathew, *Learning to Work in Groups*, Teachers College, New York, 1959. A practical handbook on group work for teachers, containing specific instructions and a good bibliography.

Parnes, S. J., and H. F. Harding, *A Sourcebook for Creative Thinking*, Scribner, New York, 1962. Twenty-nine articles by researchers, theoreticians, and practitioners provide a thorough introduction to all aspects of the development of the creative processes.

Perls, F. S., R. F. Hefferline, and P. Goodman, *Gestalt Therapy: Excitement and Growth in the Human Personality*, Dell (paperback), New York, 1965. This book contains a section of exercises for the reader to do to experience and grow in ways described in the second half of the book devoted to theory.

Psychological Films, Inc., 189 North Wheeler Street, Orange, Calif. Has a variety of films on different methods of therapy, group experience, etc.

materials for use with students:

The examples here suggest the diversity of materials available to the teacher who is interested in encouraging the personal growth or process education of his students. They range over a variety of ages, subject matters, and approaches, and care should be taken to examine them carefully to make sure they are appropriate for a particular class.

Alschuler, Alfred, James McIntyre, and Diane Tabor, *How to Develop Achievement Motivation: A Course Manual for Teachers*, Education Ventures, Inc., Middletown, Conn., 1969. A self-instructional course for teachers who want to help students set goals for their own achievement and develop a "motive pattern" which will help them get there.

Anthropology Curriculum Project, *A Sequential Curriculum for Anthropology for Grades 1–7*, University of Georgia, Athens, Ga. Introduces students to concepts and tools of the anthropologist's approach to the basic questions about man. The unit on language takes an information processing approach to linguistics.

American Association for the Advancement of Science, *Science: a process approach*, AAAS Misc. Publication 65-27, 1965. This extensive K–6 course teaches such scientific processes as hypothesizing, predicting, and controlling variables, using whatever scientific content best illustrates the process. By using some of the methods suggested in this book, the teacher can broaden this process approach so that it applies to personal growth as well as scientific content.

Barth, Roland, and Charles Rathbone, "Informal Education," *The Center Forum*, July, 1969, published by The Center for Urban Education, 105 Madison Ave., New York. An extensive, annotated bibliography on the "Leicestershire movement," or "integrated curriculum," an educational program which provides a wide variety of materials and problem exercises so that children have the freedom to choose much of the direction and pace of their own learning. Most material is elementary level, but the principles are applicable at all levels.

Bessell, Harold, and Uvalo Palomares, *Methods in Human Development*, Human Development Training Institute, 4455 Twain Ave., San Diego, Calif., 1967. A program for primary and early elementary school, providing structured group experiences that give students self-confidence, a sense of mastery, and the skills to help each other.

"Big Rock Candy Mountain," 1115 Merrill Street, Menlo Park, Calif. Available Fall, 1970. Extensive catalog containing sources, reviews, and graphics describing educational materials, ideas, and environments related to personal growth and process education.

Borton, Terry, "Poetry, Like It or Not," Educational Activities, Inc., Freeport, N.Y., 1966. A long-playing record with teacher's manual. The record contains a number of fun and noisy poems designed to "grab" students. The poems are read with a class, and their comments are used to introduce or follow the poems. Middle and high school level.

Borton, Terry, Lynn Borton, and Mark Borton, *My Books*. Publishing rights under negotiation. For information, write Office of Affective Development, Board of Public Education, 21st and the Parkway, Philadelphia, Pa. A series of twenty supplementary readers that speak directly to a student's basic concerns. Physical activity, drawing, role plays, and programmed open questions involve the student in making his reading books his own.

Borton, Terry, Norman Newberg, and Joan Newberg, "All's Fair in Love and War," Educational Activities, Inc., Freeport, N.Y., 1968. A long-playing record with teacher's manual. This record contains a variety of poems, some easy and some extremely complex, on the two subjects of love and war.

Brown, George, *Now: The Human Dimension*, Esalen Publications, Big Sur, Calif., 1968. A report on a training program for teachers which combined cognitive and affective learning to create a "humanistic education." Janet Lederman's *Anger and the Rocking Chair*, McGraw-Hill, New York, 1969, describes in a prose poem how one of the program's teachers used gestalt awareness with children. All levels.

Brooks, Charlotte, and Lawana Trout, *The Impact Series*, Holt, New York, 1968. A series of high school English books dealing with personal concerns of adolescent students, with particular emphasis on city populations.

Burgess, Bonita, "A Bibliography for a Human Development Curriculum," Intensive Learning Center and Office of Affective Development, Philadelphia Public Schools, Intensive Learning Center, 15th and Luzerne Streets, Philadelphia, Pa. Extensive information on both adult and children's materials (books, films, stories, records) appropriate for developing the human potential of elementary children. Sources for instructional materials are listed. Emphasis on intergroup relations.

Burgess, Bonita, "A Working Bibliography on Games," Intensive Learning Center and Office of Affective Development, Philadelphia Public Schools, Intensive Learning Center, 15th and Luzerne Streets, Philadelphia, Pa. Describes games, sources of games, and background discussions on how games may be used to teach thinking processes. A curriculum outline is being developed.

Covington, Martin, et al., *The Productive Thinking Program*, Educational Innovation, Inc., Box 9248, Berkeley, Calif. A course using programmed learning in comic book detective mysteries to teach problem-solving processes, or "master-thinking skills." Middle school level.

DeMille, Richard, *Put Your Mother on the Ceiling*, Walker, New York, 1967. A series of exercises in creative thinking with, as the title suggests, a droll and fanciful bent. Useful for encouraging the use of fantasy at almost any level.

Doubleday and Company, Inc., *Unfinished Stories*, Garden City, N.Y. A series of short color films which depict a conflict of conscience and then leave it up to the audience to decide what should be done. The attention to the difference between *knowing about* what should be done and actually *doing* it makes it easy to give these films a process emphasis. Printed versions of the stories are available from the National Education Association, Publications-Sales Section, 1201 Sixteenth Street, Washington, D.C. Middle school level.

Educational Development Center, "Man: A Course of Study," 15 Mifflin Place, Cambridge, Mass., 1968. An elaborate course based on the ideas outlined by Jerome Bruner, "Man: A Course of Study" attempts to answer the question "What is human about human beings?" by contrasting life in America with the lives of animals and of Eskimos. Includes documentary movies shot on locale, artifacts, teacher guides, etc.

Gibson, John, *The Intergroup Relations Curriculum: A Program for Elementary School Education*, vols. 1 and 2, Tufts University Press, Medford, Mass., 1969. Contains specific lesson plans covering overall program, ways of dealing with different cultures, decision making, group processing, racial differences, etc. Research results and general discussion are extensive.

Jaynes, Ruth, and Barbara Woodbridge, *Bowman Early Childhood Series*, Bowman Publishing Co., Glendale, Calif., 1969. A series of picture stories, story books, and recordings designed to develop positive self-identity, awareness of self as a person, motor-perceptual skills, and ability to relate to others.

Lippet, Ronald, Robert Fox, and Lucille Schaible, *Social Science Laboratory Units*, Science Research Associates, Inc., 259 East Erie Street, Chicago, Ill., 1969. Teacher's guide, resource book, records, and student materials for an experiential and intellectual look at human behavior as seen through the eyes of a social scientist. Middle school level.

Medeiros, Vincent, *The Voices of Man Literature Series*, Addison-Wesley Publishing Co., Menlo Park, Calif. A high school literature series for disadvantaged students combining literary merit and relevance to the students' own concerns.

Moffet, James, *A Student-centered Language Arts Curriculum*, vol. 1 (grades K–6) and vol. 2 (grades K–13), and *Teaching the Universe of Discourse*, Houghton Mifflin, Boston, 1968. A comprehensive English program centered around the students themselves and the kind of discourse—drama and speech—with which they are most familiar. Specific lesson plans and exercises are given.

Muessig, Robert, *Discussion Pictures for Beginning Social Studies*, Harper and Row, New York, 1967. Ninety large pictures on such basic human themes as the unity and diversity of man and man's search for security. Primary level, but useful in many contexts.

Newberg, Norman, and Terry Borton, *Education for Student Concerns*, Office of Affective Development, Philadelphia Board of Education, 21st and the Parkway, Philadelphia, Pa. Process courses in communications and urban affairs, together with extensive theoretical introduction, teacher-training materials, and anthologies of student readings for each course. The courses and anthologies are still in developmental stages, but descriptive materials and sample lessons are available. High school level.

Northwest Regional Educational Laboratory, "Information on Program 100," 710 S.W. Second Ave., Portland, Oregon, 1969. Describes various course materials now being developed to teach "generic processes" for higher-level thinking abilities, questioning strategies, interpersonal communication, and problem solving. All levels.

Oliver, Donald, and Fred Newman, *Public Issues Series*, Xerox Corporation, Education Center, Columbus, Ohio. A series of pamphlets on such topics as "Status," "The Civil War," and "Science and Public Policy" present materials which raise basic questions in the social studies area. Emphasis is placed on teaching the processes of productive discussion, particularly in the pamphlet, "Taking a Stand." High school level.

Orme, Michael, and Richard Purnell, "Behavior Modification and Transfer in an Out-of-Control Classroom," Center for Research and Development on Educational Differences, Harvard University, Cambridge, Mass., 1968. Though basically a research report, this paper does contain a description of the use of behavior modification techniques in the classroom. A more extensive discussion is in Albert Bandura's *Principles of Behavior Modification*, Holt, New York, 1969.

Randolph, Norma, and William Howe, *Self-enhancing Education: A Program to Motivate Learners*, Stanford, Stanford, Calif. A book of specific procedures for teaching kids to learn more about how to control themselves, direct their own learning, and create their own selves. Directed toward teachers dealing with elementary students. Based on programs developed in Cupertino, Calif.

Raths, Louis, Merill Harmin, and Sidney Simon, *Values and Teaching*, Charles E. Merrill Books, Inc., Columbus, Ohio, 1966. A concrete approach to the teaching of value clarification, including many exercises suitable for any level.

Shaftel, Fannie, and George Shaftel, *Words and Actions: Role-playing Photo-problems for Young Children*, Holt, New York,

1967. Uses roleplays centered around such problems as spilled groceries, disagreement with parent on shoe styles, fight over blocks, etc., to teach young children to recognize and deal with their feelings. One set of pictures raises problems common in entering a new school situation. Urban emphasis.

Smiley, Marjorie, *Gateway English*, Macmillan, New York, 1966. High school English series dealing with themes such as "Who am I?" and "Coping."

Spolin, Viola, *Improvisation for the Theater*, Northwestern University Press, Evanston, Ill., 1963. A sequential program for teaching improvisation, containing exercises which can be easily adapted for many classroom activities.

Straus, David, et al., *Tools for Change*, Interaction Associates, 2637 Rose St., Berkeley, Calif. A course outline for a program which explicitly teaches problem-solving processes through the use of games and puzzles. All levels.

Synectics, Inc., *Making It Strange*, Harper & Row, New York, 1968. A four-book series designed to teach children to be more creative. The books also lend themselves well to an exploration of the inner life out of which creativity springs.

Tannen, Robert, *I Know a Place*, City Schools Curriculum Service, Inc., 60 Commercial Wharf, Boston. A series of booklets provide open questions and the opportunity for children to help write their own book as they explore their relation to their environment. Elementary level.

Wight, A., *Cross-Cultural Training: A Draft Handbook*, Center for Research and Education, P. O. Box 1768, Estes Park, Colo., 1969. Though it focuses on the training of Peace Corps volunteers, this book contains a number of lesson outlines which can easily be adapted for school use, particularly in a crosscultural or integrated setting.

index

209